THE FINAL FLIGHT
JUMPS GUIDE 2015/16

GRANT COPSON & LEE LEWIS

Published by CreateSpace

© Copyright Grant Copson & Lee Lewis 2015

© Copyright Cover Design Francessca Webster 2015

ISBN – 978-1516860579

THE FINAL FLIGHT JUMPS GUIDE 2015/16

Photographs of UK trained horses inside this publication have been supplied by Michael Harris. Facebook page: Harris Equine Photography, Twitter account: @mjyharris and on his Instagram account: Michael Harris. Photographs of Irish trained horses inside this publication have been supplied by Dan Heap, website: wbyhorseracingphotography.com.

Produced by The Final Flight Publications LLP. 158, Homefield Road, Sileby, Loughborough, Leicestershire. LE12 7TQ.

Email: thefinalflightpublications@outlook.com

Website: www.thefinalflightpublications.com

All information is deemed correct at the time of going to press. However, no responsibility is accepted by the publishers, for any error or their consequences.

MAIN FRONT COVER IMAGE: DOUVAN (Ruby Walsh) wins the 2015 Grade 1 Champion Novices' Hurdle at the Punchestown Festival. Image supplied by Dan Heap.

BACK COVER IMAGE: Nicky Henderson's Seven Barrows stables. Image supplied by Michael Harris.

CONTENTS

INTRODUCTION

Welcome to the first edition of The Final Flight Jumps Guide. Firstly, thank you for buying this publication and we hope that you find it a useful source of information for the coming National Hunt season. We have been enthusiastic fans of National Hunt racing for many years and this has given us the inspiration, commitment and in-depth knowledge that we feel is essential when writing a racing form guide.

The 40 top prospects have been selectively assembled and we are hopeful that they will yield a profit over the course of the season. Although this section includes horses from the top British and Irish stables, we have attempted to highlight some horses with lower-profile connections, who we feel have the ability to compete in some of the season's top races. The handicap section is made up of horses that we feel have been allotted a lenient handicap mark based on their form to date. Where possible we have attempted to highlight potential targets for the selected horses but regardless of where they run, we feel that they should all be capable of progressing further this season. An insight into some of the most impressive point-to-point horses from last season is sure to prove an interesting read and we hope that there is plenty of bumper and hurdle winners to follow in this section.

Following the tragic death of chasing legend Kauto Star over the summer, we felt it was fitting to write a tribute to a horse that has left both of us and many other National Hunt fans with so many happy memories. Our analysis of the Champion Hurdle, Champion Chase, World Hurdle and Gold Cup should prove informative, reminding you of last season's results and more importantly giving you our opinions on this season's renewals.

We would like to say a special thank you to our photographers Michael Harris (UK) and Dan Heap (Ireland) for their contributions to The Final Flight Jumps Guide 2015/16.

Finally, we wish you the very best of luck for the coming season.

Grant Copson & Lee Lewis

40 TOP PROSPECTS

ANIBALE FLY (FR) 5-y-o b g

Assessor (IRE) – Nouba Fly (FR) (Chamberlin (FR))

Trainer: A J Martin   *Owner (s): John P McManus*

Form Figures: 211-   *Novice Hurdler (2m4f – 3m)*

The Final Flight Analysis

A runner-up to the talented Jetstream Jack at Fairyhouse on debut was a nice introduction for this son of Assessor, where the front pair pulled a long way clear of the third. He caught the eye of leading owner JP McManus and subsequently changed hands post-race to continue his career in the famous green and gold hoops. Navan was the destination of his second outing, where he quickened up nicely in the home straight to run out a convincing winner in the end. Anibale Fly's final race of the season came in a good bumper at Fairyhouse, which included Champion Bumper runners, Livelovelaugh and Au Quart De Tour as well as Gordon Elliott's talented Space Cadet. He travelled powerfully throughout the race and with approximately two furlongs to race, he began to pick up and stayed on well inside the final furlong to score by a comfortable 1 ¼ lengths.

Tony Martin's gelding has some smart form in the book, clocking some exceptional sectional times in his two bumper wins and it is hard to not be impressed by the manner in which he is able to finish his races. He appears to be a genuine individual, finding plenty for pressure, which will stand him in good stead when he attempts to compete at a higher level in the coming season. The manner of his final two victories is a sign that he has plenty of stamina and there appeared to only be one horse still galloping at the finish on his latest start at Fairyhouse. It is expected that his connections will attempt to win a maiden hurdle before stepping him up in class and we feel that he will be best suited by 2m4f, bringing his stamina into play. He looks a lovely horse for the future.

ANOTHER BILL (IRE) 5-y-o ch g

Beneficial – Glacier Lilly (IRE) (Glacial Storm (USA))

Trainer: Nicky Richards   Owner (s): Langdale Bloodstock

Form Figures: 11-   Novice Hurdler (2m – 2m5f)

The Final Flight Analysis

A son of Beneficial who cost his connections €50,000 at Tattersalls in August 2013. He managed to live up to expectations, remaining unbeaten in bumpers for Nicky Richards. Both of his wins to date have come at Ayr, the first over 1m5f in November. He travelled strongly under Brian Harding and galloped all the way to line to win by 2 ¼ lengths, beating next time out winner, Verona Opera. It was most impressive that Another Bill was giving away 23lbs to the runner-up and was still able to win in such comfortable fashion. His second win was over 2m, where he was again able to give away weight and beat another next time out winner, Baby Bach. This time he was giving away 10lb and won by a head but the front pair pulled 28 lengths clear of the third. Although he was only a narrow-margin winner, it is possible that the heavy ground and extra 10lb took its toll in the closing stages.

Another Bill is one of the most interesting horses in this section and with further progress likely when switched to hurdles, he should prove well worth following in the coming season. His wins to date have come on good to soft and heavy going and this is no surprise, with his rounded action certain to be suited by some ease in the ground. He still needs to grow into his big frame and for that reason it is expected that another summer at grass should do him the world of good. His owners are renowned for buying and selling and there will be plenty of interested parties in this talented individual if connections opt to send him to the sales. His handler will certainly be hoping that Another Bill remains in his care as he looks one of the most exciting novice hurdle prospects in the North.

AUX PTITS SOINS (FR) 5-y-o gr g

Saint Des Saints (FR) – Reflexion Faite (FR) (Turgeon (USA))

Trainer: Paul Nicholls   *Owner (s): J Hales*

Form Figures: 1/311-   *Novice Chaser (2m4f – 3m)*

The Final Flight Analysis

A 5-year-old who was twice a winner at Auteuil before joining Paul Nicholls. He was given a huge task on his British debut, taking on experienced handicap hurdlers in the 2m5f Coral Cup at the Cheltenham Festival. However, Aux Ptits Soins justified his trainer's decision, defying a mark of 139 and two significant errors, to land the prize in fine style. The fourth placed horse, Taglietelle, has franked the form since by winning a valuable handicap hurdle at Aintree and it is hard to believe that there is not a lot more improvement to come from this John Hales-owned gelding.

Aux Ptits Soins only start in Britain during the 2014/15 season was the Coral Cup and that was surprising given the talent that he possesses. He has the ability to compete in Graded hurdles but Nicholls is a master with this type and it is likely that he has a plan geared around a novice chase campaign for the coming season. He appears to have plenty of scope for that game and given his dam is a half-sister to Irish Hennessey winner Quel Esprit, he should excel when switching to the larger obstacles. The champion trainer has an excellent record with chasers and his British debut victory proved that he has what it takes to go right to the top over fences. Although he will make up into a staying chaser in time, he is expected to be campaigned between 2m and 2m4f in the early part of the season as he seems to have plenty of speed. It was made publically aware that Nick Scholfield said he was the best horse he had ever sat on leading up to his British debut and although homework doesn't always tell you the full story, this is very high praise from the talented young jockey. French recruits often come to Britain with big reputations, so it would have pleased Nicholls that this horse was able to justify the positive vibes. He is a very exciting prospect for the coming season.

BEAT THAT (IRE) 7-y-o b g

Milan – Knotted Midge (IRE) (Presenting)

Trainer: Nicky Henderson   *Owner (s): Michael Buckley*

Form Figures: 26/121/16-   *Novice Chaser (2m5f – 3m)*

The Final Flight Analysis

A smart novice hurdler during the 2013/14 season, Nicky Henderson's gelding was fully-expected to take high rank as a staying hurdler or novice chaser last season. Unfortunately, he was only able to make one appearance during the 2014/15 campaign, where he was well beaten in a 2m4½f hurdle at Cheltenham. However, he clearly needed the run that day and therefore his effort can be excused. As a novice hurdler, stamina proved to be his forte, with his best two performances coming when he easily brushed aside 2015 World Hurdle hero Cole Harden at Aintree before beating 2015's excellent RSA winner Don Poli at the Punchestown Festival. With this in mind, he is likely to improve again when stepped up in trip once more.

It is assumed that connections will now opt to send Beat That chasing, where he should get plenty of opportunities to bring his stamina into play. He has only had five runs over hurdles and looked a real progressive individual as a novice hurdler. He is a horse that has a huge frame and it is hoped that he has developed physically over the summer, allowing him to realise his full potential. This horse has displayed that he has battling qualities to go with his unquestionable class, two attributes that are required to make a top-class staying chaser. He has always looked a three-mile chaser of the future and connections were understandably excited to put this one away after his Punchestown victory. As long as he has managed to get over any problems that restricted him to only one run last season, Beat That should prove to be one of the best novice chasers in the staying division. If things go to plan, the RSA chase could be the end of season target, a race that his trainer Henderson has won twice with Trabolgan and Bobs Worth.

BELLSHILL (IRE) 5-y-o b g

King's Theatre (IRE) – Fairy Native (IRE) (Be My Native (USA))

Trainer: W P Mullins   *Owner (s): Andrea & Graham Wylie*

Form Figures: 2/1202-1   *Novice Hurdler (2m – 2m5f)*

The Final Flight Analysis

Willie Mullins' gelding was a winner on his debut under rules at Thurles after finishing second in his sole point. He then faced the previous season's Champion Bumper fifth Vigil at Leopardstown in December, where he was beaten but showed plenty of promise as he was giving the winner 4lb. Mullins' runners disappointed in the Champion Bumper but Bellshill, a well beaten tenth, was the best finisher for Ireland's champion trainer. At Aintree, he bumped into a very useful horse in Barters Hill, where he finished an encouraging second and the front pair were a fair way clear of the third. He may have just got out battled in the closing stages that day and on another day he could easily have been successful. He made amends for his narrow defeat at Aintree in the Punchestown Champion Bumper, running out an impressive winner. Patrick Mullins kicked for home off the final bend and from there, the result never looked in danger. He reversed the form with Modus, who was second at Cheltenham but only managed third at Punchestown and Bellshill proved that his Cheltenham running was not a true reflection of his ability.

Most form students could have written off Mullins' contingent of bumper horses before Aintree and Punchestown but Bellshill proved a really progressive individual and is certain to have altered the opinion of many. He appeared to come on for each run last season and he should continue to do so over timber this term. Based on his smart bumper form, a smooth transition to hurdles is expected and Bellshill is likely to be one of the leading lights for the Mullins stable in 2015/16. He has a similar profile to his connections smart-hurdler Shaneshill and we expect that either the Supreme Novices' Hurdle or Neptune Novices' Hurdle are likely to be his festival target.

11

Bellshill looks a real bright novice hurdle prospect for Willie Mullins next season. Pictured here winning the Champion Bumper at the Punchestown Festival last term.

BARTERS HILL (IRE) 5-y-o b g

Kalanisi (IRE) – Circle The Wagons (IRE) (Commanche Run)

Trainer: Ben Pauling   Owner (s): Circle Of Friends

Form Figures: 1111-   Novice Hurdler (2m – 2m5f)

The Final Flight Analysis

Unbeaten in bumpers, Barters Hill did nothing but improve throughout his first season. He was a shock 25/1 winner on his racecourse debut, defeating the ultra-consistent Simply Rouge before successfully defying a penalty at Warwick. A Listed event at Newbury was Barters Hill's next assignment, a significant step-up in class. Turning into the straight there were a number of horses queuing up to challenge him but Barters Hill denied all of his rivals to win in gutsy fashion, proving he has the class to match his excellent attitude. Connections decided to swerve the Champion Bumper, opting to let him take his chance in the Aintree equivalent instead. He rounded off a magnificent campaign to get the better of Bellshill in a gruelling battle up the Aintree run-in, the pair pulling 12 lengths clear of the third. This was another improved effort, with Bellshill boosting the form when winning the Punchestown Champion Bumper.

This horse is extremely difficult to pass, dominating his races from the front and is sure to prove a lovely recruit to novice hurdles for his connections. It was reported that he went from being the worst work horse, to a horse that none of his stablemates can live with and it is understandable that Ben Pauling is really excited to send him over timber. He is likely to start his hurdles career over the minimum distance but a step up in trip is sure to bring out further improvement. He looks as though he will handle most ground conditions and will certainly not be inconvenienced by winter ground with his win at Newbury coming on soft ground. He should prove himself as a Graded performer over hurdles this season and the Challow Novices' Hurdle at Newbury in January is a likely target, a race that will probably form his plans for the spring.

BITOFAPUZZLE 7-y-o b m

Tamure (IRE) – Gaelic Gold (IRE) (Good Thyne (USA))

Trainer: Harry Fry   Owner (s): Chris Giles & Potensis Bloodstock Ltd

Form Figures: 11/112131-   Novice Chaser (2m4f – 3m)

The Final Flight Analysis

An outstanding 7-year-old mare trained by one of the most promising up and coming trainers in Harry Fry. She started last season in a Listed bumper at Cheltenham, where she was mightily impressive to fend off speedier rivals, winning by 3 lengths. She was switched to hurdles following her Cheltenham success and was equally impressive, finishing in the frame on all of her five starts including three wins, a second and a third. After her maiden hurdle success and a narrow margin defeat in a 2m4f Listed hurdle, she was upped in trip and this appeared to bring out further improvement. She showed a nice attitude to deny multiple hurdles winner Carole's Spirit and proved why she is held in extremely high regard by her handler. Her second defeat of the season came in the Mares Hurdle at Cheltenham, where she was beaten ½ a length behind Glens Melody. Her final start was in the Mares Novices' Hurdle Final at Fairyhouse, where she slammed subsequent Grade One winner Petite Parisienne, by an easy 4 ½ lengths. She won this in the form of a stayer, as she was sent into the lead a long way from home and she was value for more than the eventual winning margin.

This mare has shown what she is capable of on numerous occasions, especially on her final start where the 2m4f trip was far from her ideal racing distance. She has plenty of scope to tackle the larger obstacles and it is expected that this is the route that connections will opt for in the coming season. There are not many mares that can compete with the opposite sex but Bitofapuzzle is a really exciting novice chase prospect and it would be no surprise if she was able to pick up some decent prizes throughout the 2015/16 campaign. She has proven that she stays 3m well and that looks to be the trip where she is likely to excel over.

Bitofapuzzle ran a fine race to be third in last season's Mares Hurdle and still has plenty of scope for improvement over fences.

BORN SURVIVOR (IRE) *4-y-o b g*

King's Theatre (IRE) – Bob's Flame (IRE) (Bob Back (USA))

Trainer: Dan Skelton   Owner(s): Mrs G Widdowson & Mrs R Kelvin-Hughes

Form Figures: 1-   Bumper / Novice Hurdler (2m – 2m5f)

The Final Flight Analysis

A winner of his sole Irish point, a 4-year-old maiden at Broughshane over 3m in April 2015. He showed a great turn of foot in that race and was eased down on the run-in to win comfortably by 2 ½ lengths. Given a confident ride by Jamie Codd, he travelled well throughout the race and sprinted clear on the run in to score in impressive fashion. Arguably, he could have won by a lot further in the end, creating an excellent impression and looks a horse with a bright future. The form of the race is working out well with the fourth and sixth placed horses winning since. Following his impressive point-to-point victory, he was subsequently sold at Brightwells in April for £220,000 and was switched to Dan Skelton's yard.

This son of King's Theatre looks an ideal type for jumping and for that reason he may only contest one or two bumpers before being switched to hurdles. After the sales it was reported that his new connections loved his scope and believe that he is a similar type to their multiple-hurdles winner Different Gravey. He is the type that will make up into a lovely chaser in time but he is certain to be capable of paying his way in bumpers and over timber before switching to that code in the future. The fact that his sole point was run at a steady gallop, where he managed to quicken-up in such impressive fashion, proves that he possess plenty of speed and therefore there is no reason why he should not be campaigned in bumpers and novice hurdles over the minimum distance. He has an excellent National Hunt pedigree, is in good hands and he looks a really exciting long-term prospect for his new connections.

CHAMPERS ON ICE (IRE) 5-y-o gr g

Robin Des Champs (FR) – Miss Nova (Ra Nova)

Trainer: David Pipe   Owner (s): Professor Caroline Tisdall & Bryan Drew

*Form Figures: **U1**-1   Novice Hurdler (2m4f – 3m)*

The Final Flight Analysis

This son of the popular Robin Des Champs cost £205,000 at Brightwells in March following a comfortable success in his second point-to-point. David Pipe was keen to run this 5-year-old under rules and opted for a bumper at the Punchestown Festival as his first assignment. As expected, this was a fiercely contested event and Champers On Ice showed tremendous battling qualities to see off another useful prospect and subsequent Galway Festival winner First Figaro in a close finish. He was ridden positively by Jamie Codd, racing up with the pace throughout and displayed an excellent attitude to get back up in the final strides after being headed inside the final furlong. The front pair pulled 28 lengths clear of the third and with that horse previously winning his only point-to-point start, the form looks solid.

It is assumed that connections will opt to switch Champers On Ice to hurdles and judged on his debut effort, he ought to make up into an excellent recruit to that sphere. He looks like the type that will relish a step-up in trip in the future and it would be no surprise if he shows his best form over 3m when switched to jumping. Pipe's gelding won his point-to-point on soft ground and following his successful rules debut, he looks like a horse that will appreciate a bit of ease in the ground.

Over the close season, we managed to catch up with connections and they made the following comments, *"He looks a proper National Hunt type, a big rangy sort who ran a fantastic race at Punchestown, showing plenty of guts and determination. He should be a nice staying-hurdler for us this season and we are very excited about this one."*

CLEAN SHEET 6-y-o b g

Oscar (IRE) – High Park Lady (IRE) (Phardante (FR))

Trainer: Nicky Henderson   Owner (s): John P McManus

Form Figures: **1**/211-   *Handicap Hurdler / Novice Chaser (2m4f – 3m)*

The Final Flight Analysis

This lightly-raced son of Oscar is a full-brother to Nelson's Bridge who was a bumper and novice hurdle winner for the same connections. He has shown plenty of promise in his four career starts, initially in his sole point, where he was trained by Enda Bolger to beat 159 rated hurdler Kilcooley by 4 lengths. Following his impressive point-to-point victory he subsequently changed hands and was switched to Nicky Henderson's stable. He made his hurdling debut at Sandown in a novices' hurdle race and was beaten 1 ¼ lengths by useful stablemate Caracci Apache. He powerfully moved to the front after jumping the last but the winner's stamina got the better of him in the closing stages and he was narrowly denied a rules debut success. He made amends next time out by winning an above average novices' hurdle at Newbury, a race that has previously been won by high-class hurdlers Rock On Ruby and Khyber Kim. A couple of mistakes in the home straight nearly cost him that day but he battled on gamely, denying the runner-up in the final strides. His last run of the season was at Fakenham over 2m4f where he made light work of his rivals, beating the Nicky Richards-trained Chidswell by an easy 3 lengths.

He appeared to appreciate the step up in trip on his final start of last season and it is expected that he will continue to progress when racing beyond 2m4f. It would be no surprise if connections exploit his low hurdles mark of 135 before he is switched to fences for a novice chase campaign. He appears to have plenty of size and scope to make a decent novice chaser and should continue to progress with more racing experience. It is likely that he will be campaigned between 2m4f and 3m as a novice chaser, with his tough and genuine attitude a trait that is certain to help him in that sphere.

CULTIVATOR (IRE) *4-y-o b g*

Alflora (IRE) – Angie Marinie (Saberhill (USA))

Trainer: Nicky Henderson   *Owner (s): Kimmins Family And Friends*

Form Figures: 3-   *Novice Hurdler (2m – 2m5f)*

The Final Flight Analysis

A half-brother to hurdles winner Scotsbrook Cloud, this son of Alflora was only given one race last season, looking a real promising prospect on his racecourse debut, catching the eye to finish third in a decent Newbury bumper. The runners were very slowly away before picking up the pace to go a decent gallop. Cultivator was rather keen throughout the race, which resulted in him being ridden pretty handily by Barry Geraghty. He travelled powerfully into the home straight, looking the winner with 2f still to run before not picking up as well as some of his rivals. It was disappointing that he did not appear to find a great deal off the bridle but the fact that he raced enthusiastically was probably the reason that he did not quite get home and he was certainly not given a hard ride inside the final furlong.

It is expected that Nicky Henderson will opt to switch this gelding to hurdles and he looks a sure fire winner under that code. He will need to settle better to make his presence felt in the latter stages of his races and this will also give connections the option of stepping him up in trip. Although he is yet to show his full potential on a racecourse, Cultivator is a real bright prospect and should be more than capable of competing in decent company as a jumper. This is one of the darker horses included in this section but we are confident that he will pay his way in the coming season.

DISKO (FR) 4-y-o gr g

Martaline – Nikos Royale (FR) (Nikos)

Trainer: Noel Meade   Owner (s): Gigginstown House Stud

Form Figures: 1-2   Novice Hurdler (2m – 2m5f)

The Final Flight Analysis

This Noel Meade-trained grey has an excellent National Hunt pedigree and looks sure to make up into a top-class jumping prospect in the coming season. Disko, a fifth foal, is out of a dam that was placed in both of her two hurdle starts over 2m. His sire Martaline has a good record as a stallion, producing many top class jumpers including, Dynaste, Very Wood, Le Vent D'Antan and Pique Sous. On the track, Disko has proved to be very useful. His debut was extremely impressive, overcoming trouble in running to score by an easy 15 lengths. Ridden patiently in the early stages by Nina Carberry, he quickened up in fine style off the final bend, putting the race to bed within a matter of strides. His second appearance came in the Punchestown Champion Bumper, a race that included a number of more experienced rivals but he ran an excellent race to finish an encouraging second. He was slightly outpaced when the leaders kicked for home, before showing a fantastic attitude to stay on best of all, getting up for second on the line.

It is expected that this 4-year-old gelding will be sent hurdling during the coming season and based on the evidence of his first two runs, there should be plenty of improvement still to come. He looks like he has some growing to do physically so another summer at grass will do him the world of good. He is a lovely mover, has great balance and is a nice horse for Noel Meade to go to war with this winter. He looks an ideal type for the Neptune Novices' Hurdle, a race that was won in 2006 by another Gigginstown-owned horse, First Lieutenant. We expect Disko to make his presence felt in Grade 1-company before the spring festivals arrive, with races such as the Deloitte Novices' Hurdle a real possibility.

DOUVAN (FR) 5-y-o b g

Walk In The Park (IRE) – Star Face (FR) (Saint Des Saints (FR))

Trainer: *W P Mullins*   Owner (s): *Mrs S Ricci*

Form Figures: *21111-1*   Novice Chaser (2m – 2m5f)

The Final Flight Analysis

Willie Mullins appears to have another superstar on his hands in the form of Douvan. He was the emphatic winner of the Supreme Novices' Hurdle at the Cheltenham Festival in March, following two facile victories on home soil. He again confirmed the form of his Cheltenham win when he comfortably dispatched Sizing John by 7 ½ lengths in the Champion Novices' Hurdle at the Punchestown Festival.

Although he is an excellent hurdler, he has an incredible physique and it is expected that he will embark on a novice chase campaign this coming season. Douvan proved that he was by far the most superior novice hurdler last term and with further improvement likely, he is sure to make an outstanding recruit to fences during the 2015/16 season. It is important to note that Douvan achieved an official rating of 160 for his Cheltenham win, which is higher than both Champagne Fever (157) and Vautour (158). This gives the Supreme Novices' Hurdle form serious credibility, as both aforementioned horses ran with credit over fences at the following season's Cheltenham Festival. Champagne Fever was narrowly beaten in the 2014 Arkle Challenge Trophy and Vautour was an emphatic winner of the 2015 JLT Novices' Chase. His wins to date have come on varying ground and although he has already shown that he has plenty of speed by winning two Grade 1 races over the minimum distance, it would be no surprise if he appreciates a step up in trip later on in his career. Douvan will take centre stage whenever he appears on a racecourse and he looks an ideal type for the Arkle at next season's festival. His trainer has made the comment that he could be the best he has ever trained and in our opinion, he is the most exciting horse in training.

DRUMLEE SUNSET (FR) 5-y-o br g

Royal Anthem (USA) – Be My Sunset (IRE) (Bob Back (USA))

Trainer: Phillip Hobbs   *Owner (s): R S Brookhouse*

Form Figures: 11-   *Novice Hurdler (2m – 2m5f)*

The Final Flight Analysis

A 5-year-old who was successful in his sole point, a 4-year-old maiden race at Tattersalls Farm over 3m. He made all on that occasion and put in a spectacular round of jumping. The form of his point-to-point looks strong with the runner-up winning next time out in a bumper at Towcester. He was subsequently sold at Brightwells in December to Roger Brookhouse for £130,000 and switched to Phillip Hobbs' successful training operation. He was a winner at the first time of asking under rules in an Exeter bumper, beating previous Huntindgon bumper winner O O Seven. It is interesting that Hobbs has previously used this bumper in 2011 as a starting point for his smart hurdler and chaser Fingal Bay. Drumlee Sunset travelled powerfully throughout the race before quickening up well in the straight, eventually scoring by a comfortable 4 ½ lengths.

Following his successful rules debut, this son of Royal Anthem was put away for the summer and it is expected that he will reappear in the autumn as a novice hurdler. He had a tendency to hang right on his debut, proving that he is far from the finished article but he clearly has plenty of ability and is a sure fire winner over timber. He has shown plenty of speed in both his point-to-point and his bumper and therefore he looks the ideal type to start off over the minimum distance before potentially being stepped up in distance. He is an exciting hurdles prospect for his connections and may even prove good enough to compete in Graded-company. Although he won his sole point on soft ground, he looks the type that may appreciate better ground when competing at a higher level.

EMERGING TALENT (IRE) *6-y-o b g*

Golan (IRE) – Elviria (IRE) (Insan (USA))

Trainer: Paul Nicholls   Owner (s): Mr & Mrs Paul Barber

Form Figures: 1/22F2-   Handicap Hurdler / Novice Chaser (2m – 2m5f)

The Final Flight Analysis

Emerging Talent was held in extremely high-regard last season by Paul Nicholls after he was purchased following an impressive win in a Naas bumper. That day he beat subsequent Grade 2 winner Sub Lieutenant and once he responded to his jockey's urgings, he quickened up in fine style to win going away. He was sent off a warm order for his debut over hurdles, where was ridden confidently but struggled to pick up after the last and was unable to get to the winner, useful handicap hurdler Shelford. A Grade 2 hurdle at Cheltenham was his next assignment, where he was fancied to go one better than his debut effort. He again filled the runner-up spot and bumped into another smart horse, this time Nicky Henderson's Vyta Du Roc. The drop back in trip was expected to suit on that occasion but it appeared that the stamina sapping ground played to the winner's strengths and Emerging Talent was far from disgraced. Following two promising runs, his next two were disappointing as he fell when travelling well at Ascot, before being turned over at odds-on at Exeter.

Although it was disappointing that this horse was unable to register a win over hurdles, his form was franked on numerous occasions, proving that he is talented. At this stage, he looks to be on an attractive mark of 136, which connections may consider to take advantage of in a handicap hurdle. However, this son of Golan has real scope for fences and is a really exciting novice chase prospect for the champion trainer if that is the selected route. At times he has looked awkward over his hurdles, possibly impeded by his huge frame and he should be one that can really improve for the switch to fences. He looks to have little ground preference but being such a big horse, he is likely to be better suited when there is some ease in the ground.

GARDE LA VICTOIRE (IRE) 6-y-o b g

Kapgarde (FR) – Next Victory (FR) (Akarad (FR))

Trainer: Phillip Hobbs   Owner (s): Mrs Diana L Whateley

Form Figures: 1/1124011/31541-   *Novice Chaser (2m – 2m5f)*

The Final Flight Analysis

This 6-year-old proved a revelation as a handicap hurdler last term following a solid first season over timber, where he contested some of the best novices' hurdles. Due to some impressive performances as a novice hurdler, he started the season off a tough opening handicap mark of 140. After a promising reappearance off top weight at Aintree, Garde La Victoire landed the Greatwood Hurdle at Cheltenham in November, showing a fantastic attitude to deny Vaniteux by 1 ¼ lengths. He was then beaten around 7 lengths in two competitive Ascot handicaps, again off top weight, before he put up arguably his best performance of the season to beat smart-novice hurdler Jollyallan at Sandown, conceding 2lbs in the process.

It is expected that this gelding will embark on a novice chase campaign this term and he is more than capable of following in the footsteps of his owner's smart-chasers Captain Chris and Wishfull Thinking. This battle hardened performer looks to have plenty of scope for fences and being a 6-year-old, it would be no surprise if there was more improvement to come. He has been campaigned between 2m and 2m4f to date and there is no evidence to suggest that he will be stepped up in trip in the short term. Garde La Victoire's connections won the Arkle in 2011 with Captain Chris and his hurdles form has a solid enough look to warrant him consideration for that race at this early stage.

Garde La Victoire shows an excellent attitude to deny another excellent novice chase prospect Jollyallan at Sandown.

GREAT TRY (IRE) 6-y-o b g

Scorpion (IRE) – Cherry Pie (FR) (Dolpour (IRE))

Trainer: Paul Nicholls   *Owner (s): Trevor Hemmings*

Form Figures: 1/42312-   *Novice Chaser (2m4f – 3m)*

The Final Flight Analysis

A son of Scorpion who started last season off in a hot bumper at Aintree, where he was fourth behind Globalisation. He made his hurdles debut at the same venue, finishing a promising second to Ballybolley where he travelled strongly but a couple of jumping errors cost him significant ground in the home straight. His second hurdles run also ended in defeat, this time finishing third behind two smart rivals, Clean Sheet and Seven Nation Army. He again travelled with plenty of purpose before failing to have the speed to match the front pair but showed a good attitude to stick to the task, only going down by 2 ½ lengths. He managed to get off the mark over hurdles on his penultimate start of the season at Bangor-on-dee. He again showed a tendency to make jumping errors throughout the race but he showed his class by running out a fairly convincing 2 ¼ length winner in the end. His final run of the season came at Sandown in the Novices' Handicap Hurdle Final, finishing an excellent second to stablemate As De Mee. The ground was desperate on that occasion but it did not appear to inconvenience Great Try, as he galloped all the way to the line.

Trevor Hemmings owns last season's Grand National winner Many Clouds, a horse that also finished second in the Novices' Handicap Hurdle Final at Sandown and he looks to have another exciting recruit to the larger obstacles in the Paul Nicholls-trained Great Try. He looks made for that game with plenty of size and scope and therefore what he has achieved so far in bumpers and over hurdles is a bonus. He should appreciate a step up in trip as the season progresses and prove competitive between 2m4f and 3m. He is likely to be suited to races where the emphasis is on stamina, so tracks such as Cheltenham, Sandown and Ascot are sure to prove ideal.

INSPIRED POET (IRE) 4-y-o b g

Yeats (IRE) – Petralona (USA) (Alleged (USA))

Trainer: Willie Mullins   Owner (s):

Form Figures: 31-   Bumper (2m)

The Final Flight Analysis

This 4-year-old bay gelding is a very well-related individual, descending from a strong Juddmonte family. His dam is a full-sister to Eva Luna who has produced Sea Moon, Brian Boru and winning hurdler/chaser Leo Luna. Inspired Poet is a half-brother to winning pointer and hurdler Minella Rocco as well as being related to other National Hunt winners including Big Moment, Successor, Pressgang and Petrovic. He was third of seven on his debut at Horse & Jockey, interestingly carrying the same colours as the unbeaten Champion Hurdle winner Faugheen. He was sent off a warm order (5/4f), and ran an encouraging race to be beaten 3 ½ lengths by the more experienced Gigginstown-owned Polymath and that run was even better than first thought when the gelding scoped badly post-race. He made amends for his debut defeat when running out an impressive 8 length winner of a 4-year-old maiden point-to-point at Templemore. Following his win, he was purchased by Harold Kirk on behalf of Willie Mullins for £155,000. It is significant that Kirk decided to purchase this horse from William Slattery, as he has previously bought three Grade 1 winners from this vendor, Cooldine, Quel Esprit and Faugheen, all subsequently trained by Mullins.

This son of Yeats makes plenty of appeal on paper with his precocious pedigree and appears to have the ability to make a high-class jumper. It is exciting that he is in the care of Ireland's champion trainer and he can make his presence felt as a bumper horse before progressing into a novice hurdler. He will be an exciting recruit to fences in time but he should pay his way in bumpers and novice hurdles over the next couple of seasons. This horse is still an unknown quantity at this stage but it would be no surprise if he is up there with the best of Mullins' bumper crop for the coming season.

KNOCKNANUSS (IRE) 5-y-o b g

Beneficial – Dato Vic (IRE) (Old Vic)

Trainer: Michael Winters   *Owner (s): Bryan Sweetnam & Garry Brown*

Form Figures: 1-21   *Novice Hurdler (2m – 2m5f)*

The Final Flight Analysis

This gelding runs in the same colours as the very smart hurdle and chase winner Rebel Fitz. He is out of an unraced dam, who is a full-sister to multiple winner Allez Vic and is also closely related to 1995 Champion Bumper, Fighting Fifth and Christmas Hurdle winner Dato Star. A winner of his sole point at Killeagh, where he beat the well-regarded Go Long, in a race that was 7 seconds faster than the average on the day. He travelled supremely well throughout, took up the running before half way and won with a bit in hand, even though the winning distance was only 2 ½ lengths. The front pair were a long way clear of the remainder and that is usually a sign that you have witnessed two useful prospects. After his win between the flags he was sold to Harold Kirk for £180,000 but the deal failed to go through and Knocknanuss reappeared in a 2m2f Point-To-Point National Hunt Flat Race at Tipperary for his former connections. He attempted to make all, racing keenly and he was beaten by the useful Jack The Wire. He ran again two months later in a Killarney bumper and this time made amends for his previous defeat, winning in fine style by 5 ½ lengths and justifying strong market support (4/6f).

He looks likely to return to the venue of his latest win for a winners' bumper at the end of August but at the time of writing, he ranks as a nice novice hurdle prospect. Although he demonstrated that he has plenty of stamina when winning his sole point, he looks to possess enough speed to be capable of winning over the minimum distance when he is switched to timber. Ultimately his long-term future looks to be over further and he looks certain to make up into a lovely staying chaser in time. Knocknanuss is one of the darker horses in this section but he should be well worth following in the coming season.

MILSEAN (IRE) 6-y-o b g

Milan – Boro Supreme (IRE) (Supreme Leader)

Trainer: W P Mullins　　　　*Owner (s): Gigginstown House Stud*

Form Figures: 1/121/1222　　　*Novice Chaser (3m+)*

The Final Flight Analysis

Following Milsean's novice hurdle campaign, it is quite remarkable to think that Willie Mullins was able to get him to win two out of three bumpers in the previous season. This Milan gelding proved to be all about stamina over timber and that is unsurprising with his dam being an unraced half-sister to a 2m5f – 3m4f hurdle/ chase winner. He started off his novice hurdle campaign in a 2m race and was successful, beating the useful Snow Falcon by 1 ½ lengths. He was then turned over at odds-on at Thurles on two occasions over 2m4f and 2m6f, meaning that his Cheltenham Festival bid was in doubt. He was a horse that was always held in high-regard and therefore was allowed to take his chance in the Albert Bartlett over 3m where he ran a fantastic race, finishing a close second to the smart Martello Tower. He attempted to make all, setting a relentless gallop and his running-style that day meant that a number of his rivals were in trouble from a long way out. He was only headed after the last and was narrowly defeated in a gruelling drive to the line.

He has the size, scope and attitude to make a magnificent staying chaser and therefore it would be surprising if Milsean does not embark on a novice chase campaign this coming season. Although less emphasis on stamina in early part of novice hurdle campaign clearly did not help him, he is a free-going sort and appeared to improve significantly when he was allowed to dictate the pace from the front in the Albert Bartlett. With that in mind, Milsean has the ability to make his presence felt in Grade 1 races in the spring. The RSA is a race that his connections won last season with Don Poli and Milsean could prove an ideal type for that race this time around. However, he does seem to have an abundance of stamina, so the National Hunt Chase over 4m may also be considered next March.

MINELLA ROCCO (IRE) 5-y-o b g

Shirocco (GER) – Petralona (USA) (Alleged (USA))

Trainer: Jonjo O'Neill   Owner (s): John P McManus

Form Figures: **1/11-**   Novice Chaser (2m 4f – 3m)

The Final Flight Analysis

Minella Rocco, an extremely well bred son of Shirocco, won his sole point-to-point by 8 lengths, beating Taj Badalandabad and subsequently changed hands for £260,000 at Brightwells in March 2014. He was switched to Jonjo O'Neill's stable where he justified his huge price-tag with two impressive displays under rules. The first of his victories came in a Kempton novices' hurdle, where he slammed the former Nicky Henderson-trained West Wizard by 6 lengths. He then went to Newbury where he was again successful, this time at long odds-on. That day he beat Royal Vacation by 7 lengths, with the pair pulling 73 lengths clear of the remainder. He was well-fancied for the Grade 1 Sefton Novices' Hurdle at Aintree before being pulled out on the day and following this withdrawal, he was put away for the summer.

This 5-year-old gelding is a gorgeous looking horse, with huge scope and has been very professional in all of his races to date. He jumps hurdles as if he they are fences and being a point-to-point winner, he is sure to be switched to fences next term. He has shown that he has plenty of class as well as a nice turn of foot and is certainly one of the most exciting horses for JP McManus' new stable jockey Barry Geraghty to look forward to. There is no doubt that this is one of the potential stars that is included in this section as he has all of the credentials to make up into a top-class staying chaser. He looks an ideal type for races such as the Grade 1 Kauto Star Novices' Chase at Kempton (formerly known as the Feltham Novices' Chase), the Grade 2 Reynoldstown Novices' Chase at Ascot and ultimately he should be perfectly suited to the challenges of the RSA at the Cheltenham Festival.

Minella Rocco working on the gallops.

MOON RACER (IRE) 6-y-o b g

Saffron Walden (FR) – Angel's Folly (Wesaam (USA))

Trainer: David Pipe   Owner (s): Professor Caroline Tisdall & Bryan Drew

Form Figures: 1/11-   Novice Hurdler (2m – 2m5f)

The Final Flight Analysis

Following his shock 50-1 win in a Fairyhouse sales bumper, he subsequently changed hands for £225,000 at Brightwells in April 2014. He was moved to David Pipe's stable and made a successful debut for his new yard in a Cheltenham bumper in October. He was travelling supremely well at the bottom of the hill and when Tom Scudamore pressed the button turning in, he opened up a clear advantage in devastating fashion. He won by a very-easy 12 lengths, proving to any doubters that his Fairyhouse victory was far from a fluke. It was deliberated by connections whether to switch him to hurdles but instead they opted for him to reappear in the Champion Bumper at the Cheltenham Festival, where he ran out an emphatic winner. He was slowly away, which meant he was caught further back than ideal, but when the gap opened up turning in, he was still cruising under a patient Scudamore. He was asked to quicken and Moon Racer again showed an impressive turn of foot to win by 1 ½ lengths.

After establishing himself at the highest level in bumpers, this 6-year-old looks a potential superstar for Pipe and that warrants his inclusion in this section. He has the pedigree to make a jumper, being a full-brother to useful hurdles winner Saffron Wells and should progress further after only three career starts. His pedigree suggests that he is unlikely to be short of stamina, with the manner of his Cheltenham justifying that fact and therefore he also has the potential to contest races over longer trips in the future. The Supreme Novices' Hurdle looks the most likely target at this stage, a race that Martin Pipe won twice during his training career but connections are sure to consider the Neptune Novices' Hurdle as a potential back-up plan should Moon Racer prove to appreciate a longer trip.

OK CORRAL (IRE) 5-y-o b g

Mahler – Acoola (IRE) (Flemensfirth (USA))

Trainer: Nicky Henderson   *Owner (s): Mrs John Magnier*

Form Figures: 1-2   *Novice Hurdler (2m4f – 3m)*

The Final Flight Analysis

This 5-year-old gelding has plenty of stamina in his pedigree. His Dam, a winning pointer, is a full-sister to the very smart staying hurdle and chase winner Tidal Bay and also from the family of Scottish National winner Beshabar. Nicky Henderson's son of Mahler made his debut in a soft-ground bumper at Kempton. Although he showed signs of inexperience in the closing stages, Ok Corral had too much class for his rivals, winning by a comfortable 2 ¼ lengths. The form of his debut effort was given a boost when third-placed The Unit won on his next start in a competitive bumper at Newbury. He was upped in class for his second bumper at the Punchestown Festival, where he finished a promising second to the more experienced Yorkhill. He was ridden patiently by Nina Carberry but got outpaced at a crucial stage of the race, before staying on in impressive fashion to get within 2 ¼ lengths of the winner. The front pair both look exciting prospects, pulling 17 lengths clear of the remainder and there should be plenty of improvement when this horse races beyond the minimum distance over hurdles.

Ok Corral has always been held in high-regard by his connections and he looks to have plenty of scope to make up into a high-class jumper. He has been described by his handler as a 'tank' and he certainly gives the impression that he will just keep on galloping. Given his pedigree and running-style he ought to improve when he is stepped up in trip next season, with the Grade 1 Challow Hurdle at Newbury in December highlighted as a likely target. He could prove to be a really nice type for the staying hurdles as the season progresses and certainly has the ability to be a surprise package for Henderson's Seven Barrows operation. The Albert Bartlett is likely to be his end of season target, with stamina almost certain to prove his forte.

ONEFITZALL (IRE) 5-y-o b g

Indian Danehill (IRE) – Company Credit (IRE) (Anshan)

Trainer: *Phillip Hobbs*   Owner (s): *Mick Fitzgerald Racing Club*

Form Figures: *1-*   Novice Hurdler (2m – 2m5f)

The Final Flight Analysis

Phillip Hobbs' 5-year-old gelding has a fair pedigree. He is a half-brother to hurdle and chase winner Credit Box and his dam is an unraced half-sister to three bumper winners. Onefitzall was acquired by his current connections from Tom Cooper, the father of top jockey Bryan. Mick Fitzgerald Racing Club had success last season with Gas Line Boy and Cloud Creeper, who are also trained by Hobbs and it is hoped that Onefitzall can carry on the good fortunes for his connections in the coming season.

He was an impressive 15 lengths winner of his sole bumper last season at Uttoxeter. He was ridden conservatively in the early part of the race by Micheal Nolan and was still travelling well when turning into the home straight. When he was asked to quicken up, he did so in impressive fashion and won with any amount in hand. The form of the race was given a significant boost when third placed Mister Miyagi (beaten 27 lengths) won his next two starts. His bumper win was on extremely testing ground, so it remains to be seen if his winning distance was exaggerated but he could not have been more impressive. He looked a little immature on debut and therefore it would be no surprise to see him progress further after another summer at grass. Even though he is unlikely to cut it with the very best over timber, he looks a sure fire hurdles winner and is one of the lesser-known horses to be included within this section.

PEACE AND CO (FR) 4-y-o b g

Falco (USA) – Peace Lina (FR) (Linamix (FR))

Trainer: Nicky Henderson   Owner (s): Simon Munir & Isaac Souede

Form Figures: 1111-   Hurdler (2m)

The Final Flight Analysis

This Nicky Henderson-trained inmate has shown an abundance of ability in his three runs in Britain, preserving his unbeaten record in fine style. Following his debut win in the French provinces for his former connections, Peace And Co made his British debut in a Grade 2 at Doncaster, where he bolted up by 19 lengths. He then followed up in a Grade 2 at Cheltenham, where he defeated the consistent Karezak by 3 lengths. He won the Triumph Hurdle at the Cheltenham Festival on his third start for his new connections, tracking the pace throughout the race and managed to overcome a bit of trouble on the home bend. He quickened up in fine style in the closing stages to hold off the determined challenge of his stable companion, Top Notch.

Although he appears to have the size and scope for fences, he has already proven himself to be a top-class hurdler. He won arguably one of the best renewals of the Triumph Hurdle in recent years and therefore, he is expected to stay over timber for the time being. The manner in which he travels during his races and his economical jumping technique are two attributes that are required to be a top-class hurdler. It can be expected that Peace And Co will take in some of the recognised Champion Hurdle trials such as the Fighting Fifth at Newcastle, Cheltenham's International Hurdle and the Champion Hurdle Trial at Haydock before trying to emulate Katchit by winning both the Triumph Hurdle and Champion Hurdle. Although this horse has won his four races on soft ground, it is believed that Peace And Co will prove even more effective on testing ground as he matures. He is yet to encounter quicker than soft to date but connections seem to believe that he should improve significantly when encountering faster ground conditions in the future and that day is eagerly awaited.

Peace And Co moves effortlessly to post at Cheltenham on Festival Trials Day.

PETIT MOUCHOIR (FR) 4-y-o b g

Al Namix (FR) – Arnette (FR) (Denham Red (FR))

Trainer: W P Mullins　　　　　*Owner (s): Gigginstown House Stud*

Form Figures: 1-1　　　　　*Novice Hurdler (2m4f – 3m)*

The Final Flight Analysis

Petit Mouchoir is a first foal out of 2m1f – 2m3f hurdle winner Arnette. He was purchased for £100,000 in June at Goffs by Harold Kirk on behalf of Willie Mullins but interestingly he was trained by Gordon Elliott for the duration of the 2014/15 season. He won his sole point at Kirkistown by 2 ½ lengths and the form of the race has worked out well with the fourth and fifth placed horses winning subsequent races as well as the second and third being sold to high-profile connections. Even though the winning distance was only 2 ½ lengths, he was very impressive in his point-to-point after putting in a fine round of jumping. He made his rules debut in the Goffs Land Rover Bumper, a race that is often a pointer to future stars of the National Hunt game with former winners including dual Champion Hurdle winner Hardy Eustace and Newmill, a winner of the Champion Chase. He was ridden handily throughout by Jamie Codd, settling nicely in a hood, an aid that was used in both his point-to-point and bumper wins. He travelled within himself for a long way and when he was asked to quicken, the response was instant, pulling clear of his rivals inside the final 100 yards to score by a comfortable 6 ½ lengths.

Petit Mouchoir is a relentless galloper and his running-style means that he can dictate the pace from an early stage of his races. He is sure to be well-schooled before making his debut over hurdles and he is another exciting recruit to Mullins' outstanding string. He is likely to attempt to win a maiden hurdle before being stepped up in class, similarly to Milsean and Tell Us More for the same connections last season. He looks a Grade 1 winner in the making and he is most likely to be suited by races between 2m4f and 3m. Therefore, the Neptune Novices' Hurdle or the Albert Bartlett Novices' Hurdle look the most likely festival targets at this stage.

RATHNURE REBEL (IRE) 5-y-o b g

Beneficial – Euro Magic (IRE) (Eurobus)

Trainer: Noel Meade   Owner (s): Gigginstown House Stud

Form Figures: **1-**   Novice Hurdler (2m – 2m5f)

The Final Flight Analysis

This son of Beneficial, a full-brother to winning hurdler Corbally, was one of the most impressive point-to-point winners during the 2013/14 season. This well-related individual is out of a dam that is related to the smart-hurdler Limestone Lad, as well as being a half-sister to Grade 2 winner Sweet Kiln. He won his sole point, a 4-year-old maiden at Dromahane, beating subsequent Grade 2 winner Three Musketeers by an easy 10 lengths. He crashed through the first fence that day where his jockey Rob James did extremely well to remain in the saddle. The mistake appeared to take little out of Rathnure Rebel, as he continued to travel powerfully during the race. He set a blistering pace from the outset and it was most impressive that he managed to keep up such a strong gallop throughout. He steadily drew clear from his rivals to win in breathtaking fashion, creating a lasting impression on the day's racegoers. He was subsequently purchased privately by Gigginstown House Stud and is yet to been seen on a racecourse for his new connections.

We are well aware of the risks involved in including this horse in our 40 top prospects but seen as Rathnure Rebel held a bumper entry during last winter, it is assumed that Noel Meade's gelding has not had major problems and may have just been given time to mature. He is still only a 5-year-old and he has already demonstrated that he has the ability to be a smart recruit to rules racing. It is expected that he may make his debut in a bumper as a stepping stone for an imminent switch to hurdles. He is reported to be back in training this summer which is encouraging for his connections as he looks a horse with the potential to contest Grade 1 races. We are eagerly awaiting his debut and he could yet prove to be one of the most exciting horses in training.

SAPHIR DU RHEU (IRE) 6-y-o gr g

Al Namix (FR) – Dona Du Rheu (FR) (Dom Pasquini (FR))

Trainer: Paul Nicholls   *Owner (s): The Stewart Family*

Form Figures: 3310/541114/U1F121-   *Chaser (3m)*

The Final Flight Analysis

Saphir Du Rheu started the 2014/15 campaign as one of the brightest novice chase prospects in training. He unseated on his chase debut before following up with a facile success at Exeter, beating the useful Horizontal Speed by 11 lengths. He was then sent off a warm order for the Kauto Star Novices Chase (formerly known as the Feltham Novices Chase) at Kempton but fell relatively early on before the race was won by subsequent Gold Cup winner Coneygree. Due to a couple of mishaps in two of his first three chases, he was reverted back to timber and was successful in the Grade 2 Cleeve Hurdle before running a fantastic race to finish second in the Grade 1 World Hurdle. Following his fine effort at Cheltenham, he was given another chance over fences and proved why he is held in such high regard by Paul Nicholls, slamming his rivals in the Grade 1 Mildmay Novices Chase at Aintree, a race previously won by Big Buck's and Silviniaco Conti for his illustrious trainer.

Following his impressive Aintree win, it is expected that Saphir Du Rheu will remain over fences next season and can be a real superstar for his connections. This 6-year-old has the scope to be a top-class performer, especially seen as there is so much improvement in him physically and he is still unexposed as a chaser. He is likely to be carefully campaigned by the champion trainer in the early part of the season but given the opportunity, he should be able to compete in the best staying chases this term. The long term aim is sure to be the Cheltenham Gold Cup but he looks a type that would be suited by the Hennessey at Newbury or the King George VI Chase at Kempton in December so one of those may be the mid-season target. In our opinion, this horse rates as one of the most exciting horses in training.

SHANTOU VILLAGE (IRE) 5-y-o b g

Shantou (USA) – Village Queen (IRE) (King's Theatre (IRE))

Trainer: Neil Mullholland   Owner (s): Mrs Jane Gerard-Pearse

Form Figures: *11-*   Novice Hurdler (2m – 2m5f)

The Final Flight Analysis

A 5-year-old son of Shantou that changed hands for £80,000 at Brightwells in November 2014 after winning his sole point. He is a full-brother to Bun Doran, also a winner of his only start between the flags and who was also subsequently sold at Brightwells. He won his point in exhilarating fashion and the form of the race is working out well, with the runner-up and now stablemate Fingerontheswitch winning a bumper and third placed Ballykan now a dual hurdles winner. He made his rules debut in a Wetherby bumper and justified strong market support, winning in the manner of a really good horse. He travelled strongly throughout and showed a nice turn of foot to quicken inside the final furlong. It was most impressive that Shantou Village showed such a professional attitude on only his second racecourse appearance and he looks open to any amount of improvement.

Neil Mullholland's gelding looks likely to be sent over hurdles next season and based on his two starts to date, he should capable of making a smooth transition to that code. Both of his wins to date have come on good ground and his breeding suggests that he may be suited by quicker conditions, with his dam's sire renowned for producing horses that prefer quicker ground. Shantou Village appears to possess enough speed to win over the minimum distance when switched to hurdles, however it is expected that him will improve further when racing beyond 2m4f. He is a sure fire winner over hurdles and we hope that he will prove to be well worth following this winter.

THISTLECRACK (IRE) 7-y-o b g

Kayf Tara – Ardstown (Ardross)

Trainer: Colin Tizzard   *Owner (s): John and Heather Snook*

Form Figures: 3/1/517151-2   *Novice Chaser (3m)*

The Final Flight Analysis

Colin Tizzard's Thistlecrack was one of the most improved horses throughout the 2014/15 season and he is still lightly raced for a 7-year-old. He started last season in an Ascot bumper, finishing fifth behind Supasundae and Yanworth. Although he ran a decent enough race, being a stayer, he was never going to be able to do himself justice in such a hot bumper over 2m. Following the Ascot race, he was switched to timber and got off the mark at the first attempt at Wincanton. He was then upped in class and ran very disappointingly at Cheltenham, where connections stated post-race that the race came too soon after Wincanton. He bounced back to winning ways in a novices' hurdle at Ascot, where he was ridden by Ruby Walsh. He was pushed along turning into the straight but stayed on stoutly to land the spoils by a 3 ¾ lengths and was certainly not stopping at the line. He then showed incredible improvement when stepped up to 3m, winning the Grade 1 Sefton Novices' Hurdle at Aintree before finishing a staying on second in a Grade 1 at Punchestown.

Thistlecrack appears to have plenty of size and scope to jump a fence and this looks the likely route at this stage. He is extremely lightly raced over his favoured 3m trip and therefore he ought to still have plenty improvement regardless of the route connections take next season. This horse looks to have the traits of a real stayer and therefore he should be suited by a real strong end-to-end gallop. He has already proved himself to be a high-class hurdler and given the opportunity he could be an even better novice chaser this coming season. He looks the type to be suited by festival conditions and therefore the RSA looks an obvious end of season target. The World Hurdle is an option should connections keep him over hurdles.

TOWNSHEND (GER) 4-y-o b g

Lord Of England (GER) – Trikolore (GER) (Konigsstuhl (GER))

Trainer: Willie Mullins   Owner (s):

Form Figures: 21   Novice Hurdler (2m – 2m5f)

The Final Flight Analysis

A German bred son of Lord Of England who is a relatively unknown stallion but has sired a German Group 1 winner, Fendora. His dam was useful on the racetrack, successful at Listed level before being retired to broodmare duties. Townshend was unplaced in Germany on the flat as a youngster before being transferred to France, where he looked progressive on the level, but always looked in need of a stamina test. He made his hurdles debut at Angers, where he finished second to a horse that franked the form by winning on their next start. It is very exciting that this half-brother to three winners in Germany was sold for €170,000 to Harold Kirk on behalf of Willie Mullins after winning his second start, the 2m1f Prix Du Royan, a 4-year-old hurdle run at Auteuil. He travelled and jumped well throughout the race before quickening up nicely after the final flight of hurdles to beat the Simon Munir-owned favourite, Bohemian Dancer.

This 4-year-old gelding remains a novice for the upcoming season and he should make up into a top-class novice hurdler for his new connections. Similar to a lot of French recruits, he has already demonstrated that he has a real natural ability for jumping and therefore it would be no surprise if he is able to make his mark as a chaser in the future. At the time of writing, he is already relatively short in the Supreme Novices' Hurdle market (16/1) and that is understandable as his connections have an excellent record in the race with Champagne Fever, Vautour and Douvan winning the last three renewals. A maiden hurdle will be his early season target before a step up in class and Grade 1 races such as the Royal Bond at Fairyhouse and the Deloitte at Leopardstown are selected as possible targets at this stage.

TYCOON PRINCE (IRE) 5-y-o b g

Trans Island – Downtown Train (IRE) (Glacial Storm (USA))

Trainer: Gordon Elliott   *Owner (s): Gigginstown House Stud*

Form Figures: 4/111-   *Novice Hurdler / Chaser (2m – 2m5f)*

The Final Flight Analysis

Gordon Elliott's gelding that has proved himself to be a very smart bumper horse. He is a 5-year-old son of Trans Island, out of Downtown Train, making him a half-brother to the multiple hurdles and chase winner Puffin Billy. He was a promising fourth on his debut at Fairyhouse, behind subsequent Champion Bumper hero Moon Racer. He returned last season in bumpers, winning all three starts. The first was a four runner race at Galway where he beat the smart mare Rio Treasure by 2 lengths. He was then successful in another four runner event, this time at Fairyhouse, where he destroyed the Willie Mullins trained Royal Caviar by 8 lengths. Tycoon Prince was very impressive, quickening past Royal Caviar and the front pair pulled 55 lengths clear of the remainder. His final run of the season was a two runner race at Naas in which he beat Up For Review, giving the runner-up 2lb in the process. This was a very tactically run race with Up For Review attempting to make all but Tycoon Prince proved much too good, again quickening up in fine style to score by an easy 3 lengths. The manner in which Tycoon Prince put the race to bed was impressive and he galloped all the way to the line, displaying an excellent attitude.

This fine looking horse is one we rate as one of the most exciting prospects for the upcoming National Hunt season as he appears have an abundance of natural ability. It will be interesting to see whether connections opt to send him over hurdles or go straight over fences for a novice chase campaign. He is certain to make-up into a fantastic staying chase prospect in time but he doesn't lack speed and therefore he should make his presence felt in either sphere between 2m and 2m5f. Given his form and ability, it would be no surprise if he can score at the highest level in the coming season.

Tycoon Prince may have slipped under the radar but he could be one that everybody is rushing to take a photo of in 12 months' time.

UN TEMPS POUR TOUT (IRE) 6-y-o b g

Robin Des Champs (FR) – Rougedespoir (FR) (Bonnet Rouge (FR))

Trainer: David Pipe   Owner (s): Professor Caroline Tisdall & Bryan Drew

Form Figures: 333/11331321/3363-1   Novice Chaser (3m)

The Final Flight Analysis

This son of Robin Des Champs was an expensive purchase back in November 2013 when he cost connections a reported £450,000 and was subsequently switched to David Pipe's stable. He has only raced 6 times in the UK and contested some of the best staying hurdle races last term. He reappeared in the Grade 2 Cleeve Hurdle and finished third to subsequent World Hurdle runner-up Saphir Du Rheu. He travelled well for a long way before understandably getting tired in the closing stages. Following his promising reappearance it was slightly disappointing that he was only able to finish sixth in the World Hurdle. He put up an improved effort to finish a staying-on third in the Grade 1 Stayers' Hurdle over 3m at Aintree behind Whisper and Cole Harden. Un Temps Pour Tout then won the French Champion Hurdle, showing the class that he possesses with an all-the-way victory. He won easing down in the end and in doing so, he proved to any doubters that when he gets soft ground he is a worthy Grade 1 performer.

He will be switched to fences in the autumn and should take little fuss in opening his account over the larger obstacles. Although it is most likely that he needs soft underfoot conditions to show his best form, with improvement still likely, he is sure take high-rank as a novice chaser. It is likely that the Kauto Star Novices' Chase (formerly known as the Feltham Novices Chase) will be his mid-season target, a race that his handler has recently won with both Grands Crus (2011) and Dynaste (2012). If the RSA was to come up soft, he would have a live chance but regardless of the ground conditions he is sure to be involved in the staying chases at the three main spring festivals in the coming season.

VOLNAY DE THAIX (FR) 6-y-o ch g

Secret Singer (FR) – Mange De Thaix (FR) (Mont Basile (FR))

Trainer: Nicky Henderson   *Owner (s): Mrs Judy Wilson*

Form Figures: 4111215/14253-   *Novice Chaser (2m4f – 3m)*

The Final Flight Analysis

Nicky Henderson's gelding opened his account on his seasonal reappearance last year in a handicap hurdle off a mark of 144 at Huntingdon. He beat the consistent Conquisto by 3 ¼ lengths with any amount in hand, conceding 19lbs in the process. He then faced a stiff task off top weight in the Fixed Brush Hurdle at Haydock, where his stamina was probably stretched but he still managed to finish a respectable fourth. A Grade 2 at Cheltenham was his next assignment, where he was a good second to Rock On Ruby over 2m4f. Volnay De Thaix travelled well throughout that race but perhaps lacked the speed of the winner in the closing stages. Arguably his performance of the season was a fine effort to finish fifth in the Coral Cup at the Cheltenham Festival, where he gave fellow top prospect Aux Ptits Soins 16lbs and was only beaten 6 lengths. His final run of the season was in the Grade 1 Aintree Hurdle, where he was a staying-on third behind former Champion Hurdle winners Jezki and Rock On Ruby. He raced enthusiastically and attempted to make all of the running but failed to have the speed to keep up with the front pair when they quickened in the home straight.

Volnay De Thaix looks a chasing type and he certainly has the class to make up into a useful novice chaser. He has shown plenty of ability when running well in level weight races and in top handicaps, proving that he is a consistent and genuine sort. His form shows that he is probably suited to races between 2m4f and 3m but given his ability, he is more than capable of winning over 2m as a chaser. He should be well worth following over fences and has the potential to become a Graded performer in that sphere. The JLT at the Cheltenham Festival could be his ultimate aim but he is more than capable of running-up a sequence in novice chases before then.

WELSH SHADOW (IRE) 5-y-o b g

Robin Des Champs (FR) – What A Mewsment (IRE) (Persian Mews)

Trainer: Dan Skelton   *Owner (s): Walters Plant Hire Ltd*

Form Figures: 1-   *Novice Hurdler (2m4f – 3m)*

The Final Flight Analysis

Dan Skelton looks to have another nice horse on his hands, this time in the form of the well-related son of Robin Des Champs, Welsh Shadow. He is a half-brother to 2m3f – 2m6f winner Klepht and his dam is a sister to high-class chaser Celestial Gold and a half-sister to high-class hurdler Fivefourthree. He comfortably won his sole bumper by 7 lengths, beating previous bumper winner Duelling Banjos and subsequent Southwell bumper winner Younevercall. Welsh Shadow caught the eye down the back straight by travelling powerfully under Harry Skelton but as Duelling Banjos kicked off the home bend he had a few lengths to make up and he had to be pushed along to get to the long-time leader. Once he got to the hind quarters of Duelling Banjos, he always looked like the winner and he eventually pulled clear of the field, leaving a lasting impression.

His pedigree and running style leads to the assumption that this 5-year-old will be suited by a test of stamina, which makes his winning debut over 2m½f look even more impressive. He should appreciate a step up in trip in time but clearly has the class to make his presence felt over the minimum distance when switched to hurdles. He is a fine looking horse and should be a nice chaser in time but with an imminent switch to timber likely, he is well worth following. He has shown a decent level of ability already and he could easily prove good enough to be Graded class over hurdles.

WHISPER (FR) 7-y-o b g

Astarabad (USA) – Belle Yepa (FR) (Mansonnien (FR))

Trainer: Nicky Henderson   *Owner (s): Walters Plant Hire Ltd*

Form Figures: 1/14141/331211/251-   *Novice Chaser (2m4f – 3m)*

The Final Flight Analysis

A horse with real class that was lightly raced throughout the 2014/15 campaign. He reappeared in a novice chase at Exeter in January, where he was a hot favourite to shed his maiden tag at the first time of asking. He jumped well in the main but could only manage second, 3 ¼ lengths behind Ceasar Milan. Although this was a disappointing effort, Whisper had been off the track since the previous April, looked to badly need his reappearance and the soft ground that day certainly did not suit him. Following his chase debut disappointment he was switched back to hurdles for a crack at the Grade 1 World Hurdle. He travelled well for a long way, eventually finishing fifth behind impressive winner, Cole Harden. He managed to reverse the form with that rival next time out, landing the Grade 1 Stayers' Hurdle at Aintree for a second consecutive season. Whisper again travelled strongly and showed a real determined attitude on the run in to steadily draw clear and score by 3 ½ lengths.

This former Cheltenham Festival winner (Coral Cup, 2014) has proven that he has genuine class over hurdles and with plenty of size and scope, he ought to make up into one of the best novice chasers for the coming season. Although his two victories at Aintree shows that he has plenty of stamina, he may well prove most effective at 2m4f - 2m5f over fences and the JLT at next year's Cheltenham Festival could be the end of season target. It was unfortunate that he was defeated on his chase debut but that can be forgiven as conditions were not in his favour and he should make amends this time around.

Whisper stays on strongly to land his second Grade 1 Stayers' Hurdle at Aintree.

WILLIAM HENRY (IRE) 5-y-o b g

King's Theatre (IRE) – Cincuenta (IRE) (Bob Back (USA))

Trainer: Nicky Henderson   *Owner (s): Walters Plant Hire Ltd*

Form Figures: 411-   *Novice Hurdler (2m – 2m5f)*

The Final Flight Analysis

A nicely bred son of King's Theatre from the family of Daylami and Dalakhani. He is a full-brother to the very-useful flat and hurdles winner Sesenta and his dam was a 1m4f - 2m winner on the flat. This Nicky Henderson-trained gelding made his racecourse debut at Wincanton in December 2014 on soft ground, where he only managed to finish fourth. He shaped with plenty of promise that day after running green in the early part of the race, before rallying well in the home straight. He showed dramatic improvement from his encouraging debut with an emphatic victory next time out at Kempton on good ground. He travelled powerfully, before responding well when he was asked to quicken and scored in impressive style by 17 lengths. William Henry then followed up under a penalty in an Ayr bumper, a race that Henderson won in 2010 with Sprinter Sacre. He was held together before being asked to quicken up in the straight, bounding clear of a decent looking field to score by 8 lengths, proving that he is a real nice prospect.

This is a horse that looks to have a very progressive profile following his debut at Wincanton and is one that we are extremely excited about. He appears to have learnt to settle better in his races, something that helps him to use his turn of foot to full-effect in the latter stages of his races. Although his best form to date is on better ground, the fact that he failed to settle on debut certainly hindered his chances and he should be given another chance on ground worse than good in the future. An imminent switch to hurdles is likely and Henderson appears to have another useful prospect on his hands with William Henry. He looks the type to progress further over hurdles and should compete in Graded races as the season progresses.

YANWORTH 5-y-o ch g

Norse Dancer (IRE) – Yota (FR) (Galetto (FR))

Trainer: Alan King   *Owner (s): John P McManus*

Form Figures: 1124-   *Novice Hurdler (2m – 2m5f)*

The Final Flight Analysis

Alan King's gelding made an impressive racecourse debut at Wincanton, beating the useful Urubu D'Irlande by 1 length, with the front pair pulling 28 lengths clear of the remainder. The form of this race has worked out well with the runner-up franking the form by beating the highly-regarded Gaitway next time out over hurdles. Yanworth was subsequently sold privately to JP McManus and followed up his debut success for his new connections with an emphatic victory in a Newbury bumper. Following his runaway Newbury victory, he was sent off favourite for an above-average bumper at Ascot and finished second to Supersundae. He raced keenly off a steady early gallop, travelled well into the straight but was unable to get to the impressive winner inside the final furlong. He managed to reverse the form with his Ascot conqueror in the Champion Bumper, finishing an excellent fourth. He settled better at Cheltenham off a strong gallop, racing wide turning into the straight and was ultimately unable to get to the leaders inside the final furlong.

This gorgeous chestnut gelding moves beautifully in his races, catching the eye with his high cruising speed. He looks a lovely type to go hurdling with and there should still be plenty of improvement to come having only had four races to date. He has already proved that he is capable of competing at the highest level in bumpers and should be able to do so over timber this term. It is likely that his end of season target will the Supreme Novices' Hurdle but it would be no surprise if he is suited to a flatter track and therefore Aintree's Top Novices' Hurdle, now a Grade 1 race, may be one that suits him better.

YORKHILL (IRE) 5-y-o ch g

Presenting – Lightning Breeze (IRE) (Saddler's Hall (IRE))

Trainer: Willie Mullins   Owner (s): Andrea & Graham Wylie

Form Figures: **U1**1-1   Novice Hurdler (2m – 2m5f)

The Final Flight Analysis

This son of Presenting looks another outstanding prospect for Ireland's champion trainer Willie Mullins. Yorkhill is out of an unraced dam who is closely related to 2m1f - 3m1f hurdle and chase winner Offshore Account and 2m1f - 3m hurdle and chase winner Dooneys Gate. He unseated his rider in his first point-to-point but made amends on the second occasion, scoring comfortably under Derek O'Connor. He subsequently changed hands and was sent off an odds-on favourite for his bumper debut. He was settled nicely under Patrick Mullins in the early stages before pulling himself to the front. He kicked clear in the home straight, winning without his rider having to ask him any serious questions, beating previous point-to-point winner Pause And Ponder by an easy 2 ¾ lengths. He was upped in class for his second bumper at Punchestown, where he again justified favouritism to beat the smart Ok Corral by 2 ¼ lengths. The runner-up was closing Yorkhill's advantage on the run to the line but the winner was still mightily impressive and looks more suited to the minimum distance than the staying-on runner-up.

It was impressive that Yorkhill was able to show a good turn of foot to kick clear of such a smart field, in a race that is sure to yield plenty of winners in the future. He showed a good attitude, running all the way to the line and although the runner-up closed his advantage close home he always looked comfortable. Similar to a lot of Irish-trained novice hurdlers, it is likely that he will attempt to win a maiden hurdle before being upped in class. He looks to have the ability to make up into a Grade 1 hurdler over the course of next season and with him having plenty of speed, the Supreme Novices' Hurdle at Cheltenham looks the ideal end of season target. Yorkhill is one to really look forward to and we are eagerly awaiting his hurdles debut.

Yorkhill, a gorgeous looking chestnut gelding, really made a name for himself by winning a Punchestown bumper in fine style.

ZUBAYR (IRE) 3-y-o b g

Authorized (IRE) – Zaziyra (IRE) (Dalakhani (IRE))

Trainer: Paul Nicholls   *Owner (s):*

Form Figures (Flat): 34-   *Juvenile Hurdler (2m)*

The Final Flight Analysis

This son of Epsom Derby winner Authorized is a really exciting juvenile hurdle prospect. His sire is already a successful National Hunt stallion, producing Triumph Hurdle winner Tiger Roll and a number of other smart hurdlers including multiple Grade 1 winner Nicholls Canyon. His dam is a half-sister to the very useful Zarafinya, a 1m winner and fourth in the Irish Oaks. Zubayr is bred by Aga Khan and his stock have an excellent record in the Triumph Hurdle, the championship race for juvenile hurdlers. He bred Shawiya to win in 1993, Zaynar in 2008 and Zarkander in 2011. Zubayr was a maiden in France but was not beaten far on both occasions for his former connections. He attempted to make all on his debut when he placed third at Longchamp in May, beaten 1 ¼ lengths by Clariden over 11f. Following his encouraging debut he reappeared at Longchamp and again ran a solid race to finish a close fourth, this time staying on strongly in the closing stages over 12f. He attracted plenty of attention at the sales before selling for £380,000 to Tom Malone Bloodstock and will continue his career in the care of Paul Nicholls.

Although he has raced on good ground on both occasions, it is predicted that this gelding will prove just as good when he encounters softer underfoot conditions this winter. Paul Nicholls often targets one at the Triumph Hurdle Trial race at Cheltenham in November and it would be no surprise if this horse is selected to represent the Champion trainer this time around. The Adonis at Kempton is likely to be another race that is considered before a crack at the Triumph Hurdle if things go to plan. His trainer has an excellent record in the Triumph in recent years with Celestial Halo and Zarkander both being successful and at this early stage, there is no reason to believe that Zubayr does not possess the ability to make it three.

54

THE HANDICAPPERS

BELTOR *(Robert Stephens)*

Official Rating: 143   Predicted Rating: **152**

2m – 2m5f hurdler

A useful flat racer who reached an official rating of 76 when trained on the level. He made a smooth transition to timber, winning his first two starts in fine-style. His second start was most impressive where he showed an excellent turn of foot to score by 5 lengths, with the runner-up All Yours boosting the form significantly when scoring in the Grade 1 Anniversary 4-Year-Old Hurdle at Aintree. He was too keen in the Triumph Hurdle to do himself justice and given the fact that he has only raced three times over hurdles, he is sure show further improvement in the coming season. His opening mark of 143 looks fair and although he should ultimately be good enough to contest Graded hurdles as the season progresses, races such as the Greatwood Hurdle, Ladbroke Hurdle or Betfair Hurdle are likely to be on his agenda.

Champagne West has some smart form at Cheltenham and he could prove himself perfectly suited to the Paddy Power Chase in November.

CHAMPAGNE WEST *(Phillip Hobbs)*

Official Rating: 150   Predicted Rating: **165**

3m chaser

Phillip Hobbs' charge looks an ideal type for handicap chases, with plenty of scope to progress further than his opening mark of 150. He travelled and jumped well for a long way at Cheltenham in the Dipper Novices Chase over 2m5f, before being unable to quicken with useful winner Ptit Zig, a horse that is now rated 157. His form so far points to him relishing a step up in trip and it is predicted that he will prove most effective over 3m during the 2015/16 campaign. Assuming that he has managed to get over a heavy fall on his latest outing, he can prove to be a really exciting individual for his connections. It is expected that the Hennessey will be the early season target but it would be no surprise to see him contest the Paddy Power Gold Cup at Cheltenham's November meeting, with him already showing a liking to Prestbury Park, winning two out of four starts.

CHESTERFIELD *(John Ferguson)*

Official Rating: 141   Predicted Rating: **152**

2m – 2m5f hurdler

A talented flat horse, achieving a mark of 86 in that sphere when trained by Mark Johnston. He was switched to John Ferguson's stable to pursue a hurdles career where he made steady improvement throughout the 2014/15 campaign. He has only raced five times over hurdles for his new connections and was successful in three. He looks a really progressive animal with plenty of scope to continue on an upward curve for his talented handler. He travelled with real purpose on his latest outing, hitting the front in between the final two flights of hurdles, only to take a heavy fall at the last with the race at his mercy. His enthusiastic way of racing should be suited to big-field handicap hurdles as they are often run at a genuine gallop. He begins the season off a mark of

141 and it would be no surprise to see his connections preserve his handicap mark for races such as the Betfair Hurdle or the County Hurdle at the Cheltenham Festival. He is a really exciting handicapper for the coming season.

CLONDAW BANKER *(Nicky Henderson)*

Official Rating: 121   Predicted Rating: **135**

2m – 2m5f hurdler / chaser

A horse that was held in high regard by Nicky Henderson as a bumper horse, winning at Kempton before finishing down the field in a Grade 2 at Aintree. He has shown further progress since switching to hurdles, going down narrowly to Jolly's Cracked It on two occasions, a horse that is now rated 138. He also ran well behind the highly-regarded A Vos Gardes, a horse rated 137 now and who gave the form a significant boost when running the smart Different Gravey close. Clondaw Banker will begin the season from a handicap mark of 121, a rating that seems to underestimate his ability somewhat and he should be capable of winning handicaps between 2m – 2m5f. He looks a real chasing type for the future but given the fact that he has still showed signs of inexperienced on the racetrack, it is expected that connections will try to take advantage of what looks a lenient opening mark before sending him over the larger obstacles.

COGRY *(Nigel Twiston-Davies)*

Official Rating: 135   Predicted Rating: **142+**

3m+ chaser

A fine stamp of a horse, one who has always looked a staying chaser in the making. He has only had six runs over fences and although he has fallen on two occasions, he is generally a sound jumper. He was given an almighty task on his latest start when contesting the Scottish National, a race that is a real test of stamina for such a young horse. He was running an encouraging race before coming down and it is fair to say that he may have even been involved in the finish if he had stood up. He is one to really look out for in staying handicap chases in the coming season and as long as his connections preserve his handicap mark of 135, he should be capable of landing a decent prize.

DEPUTY DAN *(Oliver Sherwood)*

Official Rating: 139   Predicted Rating: **155**

2m4f – 3m chaser

Deputy Dan is one of the most exciting horses in this section. He looked a potential star when travelling best of all in the 2014 Albert Bartlett before finishing second to the surprise winner, Very Wood. Most were disappointed when he was defeated on chase debut but looking back at the form now his 4 ½ lengths behind Virak is a solid piece of form, with his conqueror that day now rated 154. Although he has already been tried in handicaps, it is difficult to believe that we have seen the best from this 7-year-old gelding over fences and he should prove well worth following this season. He will begin the season on a 6lb lower mark over fences than over hurdles and his connections should be able to find plenty of nice opportunities for him. He has been known to make a few mistakes at his fences but if his jumping holds up, he certainly has the natural ability to compete in some of the best staying chases throughout the season.

EASTER DAY *(Paul Nicholls)*

Official Rating: 142   Predicted Rating: **156**

2m4f – 3m chaser

An extremely talented horse on his day who has often let himself down in the jumping department since being switched to fences. He showed a smart level of form on his third chase start beating subsequent 2014 RSA winner and the now 154 rated O'Faolains Boy by 2 ¼ lengths. He was travelling well in a Grade 3 handicap at Cheltenham last season before falling and was then pulled up after making a bad blunder in a Grade 3 handicap at Kempton. He is still extremely lightly raced and therefore as long he has not lost his confidence, he is open to plenty of improvement. A lot of last season's novice chasers have been given high handicap marks and for that reason a race like the Paddy Power Gold Cup at Cheltenham in November could be on the radar for Paul Nicholls' charge.

IBIS DU RHEU *(Paul Nicholls)*

Official Rating: 131   Predicted Rating: **140+**

2m2f - 2m6f hurdler

A half-brother to the very-smart hurdle and chase winner Saphir Du Rheu. He showed a real good level of form when trained in France, finishing a close second (1/2 length) to Triumph Hurdle runner-up Top Notch before impressively scoring by 7 lengths on his next outing. He has been disappointing on both of his British starts to date, finishing last of six on debut at Cheltenham, beaten 30 lengths behind Triumph Hurdle winner Peace And Co. He was fancied to make amends on his second start and handicap debut but was again well-beaten behind Fox Norton. He has looked inexperienced so far and it is expected that he will improve considerably following a summer at grass. Like his half-brother, he should develop into a useful staying hurdler and therefore he is sure to progress further when stepped up in trip in the coming season.

KING'S ODYSSEY *(Evan Williams)*

Official Rating: 131   Predicted Rating: **143**

2m4f+ hurdler

Evan Williams' gelding has showed a good level of form on all of his five runs to date. Arguably his best piece of form was when he finished 6 lengths behind the now 145 rated Caracci Apache at Sandown, a race where he was sent of the 2/1 favourite. He shed his maiden tag on his fourth hurdles start at Warwick over 2m5f, winning by a comfortable 8 lengths. With a strict form line through the Sandown race, he looks to be on a workable handicap mark and his trainer has made a habit of finding winnable opportunities for horses with similar profiles. Given the fact that he has only had five races to date, he looks like one that will continue to progress as he gains more racecourse experience.

KNOCK HOUSE *(Mick Channon)*

Official Rating: 138   Predicted Rating: **145**

2m4f – 3m chaser

A decent performer over timber who relished the switch to fences last autumn, winning two out of five starts under that code. He has already proved himself to be effective in handicaps, after putting up two solid efforts in decent events. He went down by 1 ½ lengths when attempting to give the useful Stellar Notion 4lbs at Kempton in December. He then followed-up with a fine effort to finish fifth at the Cheltenham Festival in the Novice Handicap Chase, a race that is renowned for producing future handicap chase winners. Knock House won a novice chase at Huntingdon on his latest outing by a very easy 30 lengths and he looks the type that is open to plenty of improvement when he tackles open handicaps in the coming season. It is possible that a step up in trip will suit this Mick Channon-trained gelding, so handicaps between 2m4f and 3m will be ideal.

QEWY *(John Ferguson)*

Official Rating: 141   Predicted Rating: **150+**

2m hurdler

Possibly one of the more obvious horses included in this section, boasting top-class form from last season. He is a former smart flat performer, reaching an official rating of 102 in that sphere and made a smooth transition to timber for John Ferguson last term. He followed up his debut effort by showing a devastating turn of foot to win at Newbury, beating the useful Cardinal Walter by 6 lengths. He ran a decent race to finish fifth in the Supreme Novices' Hurdle behind Douvan before again running up to form when finishing third in the Top Novices' Hurdle at Aintree. He is sure to be suited by a quickly run 2m handicap hurdle and a return to Newbury for the Betfair in February is likely. However, it would be no surprise if he surpasses expectations and becomes capable of competing in Graded hurdles during the 2015/16 season.

RELIC ROCK *(Brian Ellison)*

Official Rating: 120   Predicted Rating: **134+**

2m hurdler

A horse that has some nice bumper form including victory over the useful Fletcher's Flyer, a 2 length second to the smart Zeroshadesofgrey and a head second in a Grade 2 bumper at Aintree behind hurdle winner Ballybolley. He is yet to get off the mark over hurdles but he already boasts a useful level of form including when a promising second to Glingerburn, a horse that is now rated 149. He was fancied to shed his maiden tag over timber at Bangor, where he was eventually well beaten but this can be forgiven as the longer trip proved unsuitable that day. He bumped into a useful sort on his latest outing, the 131 rated Wilberdragon and based on the evidence so far, he looks to have plenty of scope for further progression in the coming season. His handicap mark of 120 looks extremely lenient and he looks the type that could run up a sequence in 2m handicap hurdles for Brian Ellison.

ROCK N RHYTHM *(Jonjo O'Neill)*

Official Rating: 134   Predicted Rating: **143**

2m – 2m5f hurdler

This Jonjo O'Neill trained gelding had some excellent placed form in Irish bumpers before changing hands and being switched to Jackdaws Castle. He ran behind some smart opponents including the 143 rated hurdler Snow Falcon as well as smart bumper performers Livelovelaugh and Stone Hard. He made an encouraging debut for his new connections to finish third at Carlisle before winning impressively on his next two starts by a total of 20 lengths. Rock N Rhythm looks the type to do well as a handicap hurdler, with plenty of experience sure to help him in that sphere. His handler is an expert at plotting his handicappers to win valuable contests and this gelding is sure to get plenty of opportunities as he looks versatile in terms of optimum racing conditions. He appears to possess enough speed to win over the minimum distance but it would be a surprise if he fails to show further improvement when stepped up in trip.

Third lot cooling down after morning exercise at Jonjo O'Neill's Jackdaws Castle.

SAINT CHARLES *(Nicky Henderson)*

Official Rating: 131   Predicted Rating: **140+**

2m – 2m5f hurdler

This gelding has shown steady progress in his four runs to date including when winning a maiden hurdle at Doncaster in nice style on his third career start. He bumped into the 150 rated Thistlecrack at Ascot on his latest outing, where he was beaten a very respectable 3 ¾ lengths. He looks a really nice type to go handicap hurdling with, one that looks likely to show his best form when he runs on decent ground. He is already a point-to-point winner, so significant improvement is expected from Nicky Henderson's charge when he is stepped up in trip during the 2015/16 campaign. Saint Charles looks a sure fire winner of a handicap hurdle and he should be capable of running up a sequence from his opening mark of 131.

SAUSALITO SUNRISE *(Phillip Hobbs)*

Official Rating: 144   Predicted Rating: **155+**

3m+ chaser

A really talented individual that is remarkably rated 1lb lower as a chaser than over hurdles. He was highly tried as a novice chaser last term and showed some decent form, most notably when twice a runner-up behind the smart Kings Palace. He fell on his latest outing at Kempton when still travelling well, in a race that was won by subsequent Gold Cup winner and the now 172 rated Coneygree. He has always looked made for the larger obstacles and he is sure to show significant improvement in the coming season. It is expected that Sausalito Sunrise is capable of making up into a top-class staying chaser over the course of next season and for that reason his opening mark of 144 looks extremely lenient. Although it would be no surprise if he were to contest the Hennessey at Newbury in December, he looks the type that will relish a real test of stamina and Warwick's Classic Chase in January could be a race that suits him perfectly.

SOUTHFIELD THEATRE *(Paul Nicholls)*

Official Rating: 154   Predicted Rating: **165**

3m chaser

Paul Nicholls' Southfield Theatre showed a real good level of form as a hurdler before making a successful switch to fences last term, winning three out of his five starts under that code. He ran an excellent race to finish second to the very-smart Don Poli in the RSA at the Cheltenham Festival, doing extremely well to overcome a bad mistake at the ditch at the top of the hill. His opening mark of 154 means that he will be at the top of the handicap but given that he has already proved himself capable of carrying big weights in top handicaps, including when an excellent second to Fingal Bay at the 2014 Cheltenham Festival, that should prove no burden. It is understood that Paul Nicholls' charge will be given time after cutting himself in the RSA but if he was ready in time, then the 3m2f at Newbury for the Hennessey would be an ideal starting point. Although it is predicted that this horse will make his seasonal reappearance in a handicap, he is a really exciting prospect and he may well prove good enough to win Graded staying chases.

THE TULLOW TANK *(Sandra Hughes)*

Official Rating: 149   Predicted Rating: **160**

2m4f – 3m chaser

A Grade 1 winning novice hurdler for his former trainer Phillip Fenton before finishing 3 lengths behind superstar hurdler/chaser Vautour in the Deloitte Novices' Hurdle. He was switched to the late Dessie Hughes' stable, where he was successful on his chase debut, beating the 148 rated chaser Mala Beach by 5 ½ lengths. He was disappointing on his next three starts before bouncing back to form to finish a close second to Gilgamboa in the Grade 1 Ryanair Gold Cup Novice Chase. A half-brother to 2015 Grand National winner Many Clouds, Barry Connell's gelding looks sure to excel in staying chases in the coming season. Although he may be Graded class, he can make his presence felt in races such as the Paddy Power Chase and the Boylesports Handicap Chase at Leopardstown, two races that the same connections targeted last season with Foxrock.

The Tullow Tank, a real promising handicap chaser for the coming season, makes his way to post, accompanied by Apache Stronghold.

VICTOR HEWGO *(Keith Reveley)*

Official Rating: 139   Predicted Rating: **147+**

3m+ chaser

A lightly raced 10-year-old, having only five chase starts to date. He has won two out of five races over the larger obstacles but also boasts some excellent placed form behind two Grade 1 winning chasers. He finished a close ¼ length second behind 2014 Arkle hero Western Warhorse before finishing a narrow ¾ length behind the 162 rated chaser Holywell. He was sent off the well-backed 5/1 favourite on his latest outing in a competitive handicap at Aintree but was pulled-up after making a bad mistake. He looks completely unexposed as a handicap chaser and although he is unlikely to be a Grade 1 winner, he should prove to be extremely well-handicapped from a mark of 139. His form over fences warrants him the ultimate respect in all the top handicap chases, with Wetherby's Rowland Meyrick Handicap Chase highlighted as a potential target.

Very Wood and Bryan Cooper go to post at Punchestown for a Grade 2 novice chase in November.

VERY WOOD *(Noel Meade)*

Official Rating: 147   Predicted Rating: **155+**

3m+ chaser

This former Albert Bartlett hero was slightly disappointing in his first season over the larger obstacles, only managing to win once out of five chase starts. Very Wood, a former point-to-point winner is yet to reproduce the form of his 2014 Cheltenham Festival success but he looks to be on a workable handicap mark to begin the 2015/16 season and it is hoped that he will blossom over fences this time around. He is rated 147 under that code, 1lb lower than his hurdles mark and he looks an ideal type for a staying handicap chase across the Irish Sea. He has plenty of size and scope to make up into an excellent staying chaser and his form to date points to him being all about stamina. His connections often run a few in the Irish Grand National, a race that may suit this Noel Meade-trained gelding perfectly.

WEST WIZARD *(Nigel Twiston-Davies)*

Official Rating: 129   Predicted Rating: **137+**

2m4f+ hurdler / chaser

A horse that was held in extremely high-regard following a facile debut success in a Kempton bumper in March 2013. He was strongly fancied in novice hurdles at the same venue between November 2013 and February 2015, bumping into three smart prospects, Sgt Reckless, Arzal and Minella Rocco. He then pulled-up in the Imperial Cup at Sandown but he can easily be excused that run as the ground was desperate and the gelding was clearly not suited by the underfoot conditions that day. He confirmed his early promise on his final start for Nicky Henderson when successful at Kempton over 2m5f before being switched to Grange Hill Farm to continue his career in the care of Nigel Twiston-Davies. This son of King's Theatre has an attractive opening mark of 129 and can make his presence felt in handicap hurdles if this is the route that connections opt for. He looks to have the scope to jump a fence and the newly-introduced novice handicap chase programme could prove lucrative if he is sent over the larger obstacles. He should be suited to races beyond 2m4f.

POINT-TO-POINTERS

AIR COMMAND (IRE) *5-y-o-b g Milan – Seductive Dance*

Trainer: J H Culloty

Form: **12-**

An easy winner on debut, travelling strongly before making an error two out, allowing his rivals to close his lead. The manner in which he rallied after the last to pull clear of the remainder and win by 6 lengths was impressive, especially seen as he is from a stable that rarely record first time out winners in point-to-point races. It was slightly disappointing that he was unable to justify the market support when sent off the 1/2 favourite on his second appearance. However, the slow pace that day certainly did not suit this gelding and he was only beaten by 1 length, giving the more experienced winner 5lbs. He is unlikely to make his presence felt in bumpers, with stamina being his forte but he should pay his way in staying hurdle races.

BUN DORAN *4-y-o-b g Shantou (USA) – Village Queen (IRE)*

Trainer: Tom George

Form: **1**

This full-brother to top prospect Shantou Village was extremely impressive in his sole point, a 4-year-old maiden race, powering clear of his rivals to win readily by 14 lengths. He was acquired by Tom George for £76,000 after his win between the flags, a price that may prove to be extremely good value in the long-term. It is reported that this gelding was purchased with minor issues but if his excellent handler can keep him sound, he can prove himself as a promising recruit to the National Hunt game. His brother is already a bumper winner and based on his impressive debut, Bun Doran looks to possess enough speed to score in that sphere before switching to jumping.

Promising point-to-point winner Champagne Classic is by Stowaway, the same stallion that sired point-to-point and dual Cheltenham Festival winner Champagne Fever.

CHAMPAGNE CLASSIC *4-y-o-b g Stowaway – Classical Rachel (IRE)*

Trainer: Gordon Elliott

Form: 1-

A workmanlike performance on debut ensured that he was successful at the first time of asking. He caught the eye in the preliminaries before showing an excellent attitude on the track to deny Gigginstown-owned Bull Ride by ½ a length in a 4-year-old maiden at Kilworth. He was subsequently purchased by Gordon Elliott for £100,000 at Goffs sales in April. This gelding looks to have a really bright future and should make up into a high-class staying chaser in time. Champagne Fever, also by Stowaway, won a point-to-point before going on to be successful at two Cheltenham festivals and those connected to Champagne Classic will be delighted if he is able to emulate that particular horse under rules. He looks a type that will appreciate good ground and although he is likely to need time to realise his full-potential he is exciting.

CRAZYHEART *4-y-o-ch g Alhaarth (IRE) – Buckle (IRE)*

Trainer: Paul Nolan

Form: 1-

A winner of a strongly run 4-year-old maiden at Tallow, beating Minella Awards by a neck, with the front-pair pulling a further 20 lengths clear of subsequent winner Polymath. Following his successful debut, he was purchased by Paul Nolan for £110,000 at Cheltenham's Brightwells sales. He looks a nice type to make his mark under rules but most likely as a hurdler rather than a bumper performer. Anything he achieves in bumpers or over timber will be a bonus as his future ultimately lies over fences and he certainly looks to have the raw ability to become a decent chaser in time.

DANGEROUS GAMES *4-y-o-b g Scorpion (IRE) – Cyclone's Sister (IRE)*

Trainer: John Joseph Hanlon

Form: 2-

A runner-up in his sole point, a six runner 4-year-old maiden race, finishing 2 ½ lengths behind potentially top-class Petit Mouchoir. He gave the winner a race up until the closing stages but the winner showed too much class on that occasion. Petit Mouchoir gave the form a significant boost when winning a decent bumper at Punchestown and the fourth and fifth placed horses that day have won a point-to-point since, so the form of the race looks strong at this stage. It is expected that Dangerous Games can make his mark under rules and looks a lovely prospect for his new connections. He is very well-related, being the first foal out of an unraced sister to the high-class chaser Hidden Cyclone and his sales price tag of £60,000 may well prove to be good business.

DE BENE ESSE (IRE) *5-y-o-b g Scorpion (IRE) – Benedicta Rose (IRE)*

Trainer: Evan Williams

Form: **O1-**

He made his debut in a race which was won by the smart Yorkhill at Tattersalls in December 2014. He made eye-catching headway before running out two from home and although it is difficult to say whether he would have won, he was still travelling as well as the winner at the time. He made amends for his debut disappointment when a convincing winner on his second start, jumping beautifully to score by 8 lengths. Following his point win, he was subsequently sold to Evan Williams for £75,000. Although he looks a chaser in the making, this strong travelling son of Scorpion ought to be capable of winning bumpers and novice hurdles before making himself known over the larger obstacles.

DOUNIKOS (FR) *4-y-o-b g Smadoun (FR) – Baby Sitter (FR)*

Trainer: Gordon Elliott

Form: **1-**

This gelding made an impressive debut by landing what looked an above average Punchestown point-to-point for Gordon Elliott. He showed an excellent attitude to deny Semper Invicta, who is now in training with Paul Nicholls by ¾ length. Based on this evidence, he is a lovely prospect for the future and is one that connections are sure to be excited about. It is unlikely that he will be suited by 2m bumpers as he looks like he is going to be a staying-chaser in the future and therefore it would be no surprise if we see him over hurdles sooner rather than later.

EAMON AN CNOIC *4-y-o-b g Westerner – Nutmeg Tune (IRE)*

Trainer: David Pipe

Form: **2-**

A runner-up in a competitive 4-year-old maiden point-to-point, 3 lengths behind Lisheen Prince at Oldcastle, where any hope of him getting the better of the winner was ended with a bad blunder at the final fence. David Pipe subsequently purchased this son of Westerner at Punchestown's Goffs sales for £175,000 after winning a Punchestown bumper with ex-point-to-point winner Champers On Ice. Westerner's offspring including Champagne West, Deputy Dan and Cole Harden have shown significant improvement when stepping up in trip and it is expected that Eamon An Cnoic will also be suited by trips between 2m4f and 3m. It is likely that he will start off in a bumper to gain valuable racecourse experience before switching to hurdles, where he is should excel in the staying division.

GREY STORM *4-y-o-gr g September Storm (GER) – Lady Blayney (IRE)*

Trainer:

Form: **1**

An imposing grey that was successful in his sole point at Dawstown in May, subsequently changing hands post-race for £100,000. A competitive event on paper with 15 runners going to post, Grey Storm travelled powerfully throughout and showed an impressive turn of foot to score by 4 lengths. He is a half-brother to a bumper winner and his dam, a former flat winner, is a sister to high-class juvenile hurdler, Crowded House who was second in the 1992 renewal of the Triumph Hurdle. He has a lovely pedigree with a mix of speed and stamina and ought to be capable of winning a bumper before jumping hurdles.

HAWKHURST (IRE) *5-y-o-b g Flemensfirth (USA) – Silaoce (FR)*

Trainer:

Form: 1-

A winner of his sole point at Boulta by a comfortable 12 lengths and even though his jumping lacked fluency at times, the manner in which he travelled into the race really caught the eye. He was subsequently purchased by Kieran McManus on behalf of his father and leading owner JP, topping Brightwells January sales at £200,000. This full-brother to Grade 1 winning hurdler Muirhead looks to have a real bright future under rules and we wait in anticipation on how he will be campaigned this season. He could prove himself to be another star in the famous McManus green and gold hoops.

LUCKY PASS *4-y-o-ch g Ultimately Lucky (IRE) – Fuela Pass (FR)*

Trainer: Willie Mullins

Form: 1-

A chestnut gelding who was successful at the first attempt in a 4-year-old maiden at Loughanmore. He was left clear at the last when his nearest rival fell but he looked in command at the time, creating a nice impression to win by a comfortable 14 lengths. He changed hands for £140,000 at Brightwells in April 2015 to Harold Kirk on behalf of Willie Mullins after fighting of the attentions of other interested parties including Donald McCain and Tony Martin. This horse looks to have a bright future under rules for Ireland's champion trainer and should have no problem in winning a bumper before switching to hurdles. Mullins will have a strong bumper contingent as always but it would be no surprise if Lucky Pass proved himself to be right up there with the best of them.

MINELLA ARIS (IRE) *4-y-o-b g King's Theatre (IRE) – Liss Rua (IRE)*

Trainer: Paul Nicholls

Form: F1-

This gorgeous looking son of King's Theatre made his point-to-point debut at Dromahane in a 4-year-old maiden, where he fell at the fourth last after showing signs of greenness throughout. He made amends over the same course and distance next time out to win by 2 ¼ lengths beating Barenice. He was a fortunate winner that day as He's A Gent looked to have the race won before falling at the last but this was still an impressive display by a horse that clearly needs time to grow into his huge frame. He was purchased by Tom Malone Bloodstock on behalf of Paul Nicholls for £200,000 and is a horse for the champion trainer to really look forward to. He appears to be the type that will progress with time and a test of stamina but he may have the class to win a bumper before switching to timber.

MONBEG NOTORIOUS *4-y-o-b g Milan – Borleagh Princess (IRE)*

Trainer: Gordon Elliott

Form: F1-

A faller at the first fence on his debut in a 4-year-old maiden point-to-point race at Athlacca. He made amends at the second time of asking when successful at Tralee. He travelled with plenty of purpose throughout the race and showed a nice turn of foot to quicken right away, scoring by an easy 5 lengths. Gordon Elliott purchased this son of Milan for £155,000 following his impressive victory and it looks like he has a lovely prospect on his hands for the coming season. He looks likely to make himself known as a smart staying chaser in the future but given the speed that he clearly possesses, he should have no problems in winning bumpers and novice hurdles over the minimum distance in the short-term.

NORTH HILL HARVEY *4-y-o-b g Kayf Tara – Ellina*

Trainer: Dan Skelton

Form: **1-**

A son of Kayf Tara who has proved successful as a National Hunt sire, producing some talented hurdlers including Molotov, Sign Of A Victory, Tea For Two and Blaklion. He was a winner of his sole point at Worcester before being subsequently purchased by leading owners Mr & Mrs R Kelvin-Hughes. North Hill Harvey is going to be trained by up and coming trainer Dan Skelton and should be capable of winning races under rules. He is one of the darker horses in this section but at the same time, a very interesting one.

RED HANRAHAN *4-y-o-b g Yeats (IRE) – Monty's Sister (IRE)*

Trainer: Paul Nicholls

Form: **F1-**

He made his debut in a 4-year-old maiden at The Pigeons, where he was pressing the leaders before falling at the sixth fence. He made amends on his next outing with an impressive 12 length victory at Durrow, where the hot favourite Broken Soul was a further 12 lengths back in third. He showed an excellent turn of foot on that occasion, proving that he may have the speed to win over the minimum trip under rules. He arrived at the Brightwells sales in April 2015 with a big reputation following his point win and was subsequently sold for £150,000 to Tom Malone Bloodstock. Red Hanrahan is one of the most exciting prospects that is included within this section and he will continue his development at Paul Nicholls' Ditcheat stables. His win in his second point-to-point proved that he has plenty of speed, meaning that it is likely he will be campaigned in bumpers before switching to novice hurdles. He ultimately has the potential to be Graded class in time and the sky really is the limit for this one.

SEMPER INVICTA *4-y-o-ch g Shantou (USA) – Statim*

Trainer: Paul Nicholls

Form: **2-**

Semper Invicta made an encouraging debut in a 4-year-old maiden behind the well-regarded Dounikos. He gave the winner a real race that day before showing signs of inexperience, wandering under pressure in the closing stages. He was purchased for £90,000 by Highflyer Bloodstock on behalf of successful owners Potensis Bloodstock and is another who will begin his rules career under the watchful eye of the champion trainer. After running green on his debut, he should progress further with more racecourse experience. His future ultimately lies over fences but he should make his presence felt over hurdles in the short term.

SOME ARE LUCKY *4-y-o-b g Gold Well – Foreign Estates (IRE)*

Trainer: Tom George

Form: **3O2-**

This son of Gold Well has shown plenty of promise without getting his head in front in three starts to date. He was sent off as the 6/4 favourite on for his debut and put up a decent performance to finish 6 ½ lengths behind the smart Petit Mouchoir. He was turned out quickly in an attempt to make amends for his debut defeat but unfortunately ran out when he appeared short of room. His third and final race was at Broughshane in a 4-year-old maiden point-to-point, where he again bumped into a smart rival, this time in the form of Born Survivor. He travelled well for a long way but seemed to lack the speed to go with the winner, similarly to his debut effort. He subsequently changed hands for £80,000 at Brightwells in April and will be trained by Tom George, a trainer that has previously purchased some smart types from this same vendor including Some Buckle and Some Plan. Some Are Lucky looks the type that will improve with a summer at grass and with more racecourse experience.

Although he is related to bumper and hurdles winner Empire Theatre, it remains unlikely that we will see the best of him over the minimum distance and he therefore looks one for the staying novice hurdle division before ultimately making the switch to fences.

STRONG PURSUIT 5-y-o-ch g Flemensfirth (USA) – Loughaderra (IRE)

Trainer: Phillip Hobbs

Form: F31-

This horse appeared three times in the space of three months and was successful at the third time of asking. He fell on his debut in a 5-year-old maiden before making progress on his second start to finish a promising third behind the smart Air Command at Cragmore. He then showed significant improvement to run out an impressive 15 length winner at Belclare where he made most of the running, jumped with fluency throughout and won with any amount in hand. He was subsequently purchased by Aiden Murphy for £90,000 and he looks a lovely long-term prospect for his new connections. He is unlikely to be suited by bumpers or hurdles over the minimum trip but should make up into a decent handicap hurdler over 2m4f and 3m before switching to fences.

SUTTON MANOR (IRE) 4-y-o-b g Gold Well – Nighty Bless (IRE)

Trainer: Willie Mullins

Form: 2-

This 4-year-old gelding was sent off the 11/10 favourite for his point debut and finished an encouraging second to Oldgrangewood. He made a couple of crucial errors, most notably two out where he lost plenty of ground and showed a good attitude to stick to his task in the closing stages. His debut performance was impressive enough to catch the eye of Harold Kirk, who purchased him for £125,000 at Brightwells in March on behalf of Willie Mullins.

Being a son of Gold Well, a full-brother to Montjeu, whose progeny include Holywell and John's Spirit, he is bred for the job and looks a sure fire bumper winner for his leading connections.

THEATRE TERRITORY *5-y-o-b m King's Theatre (IRE) – Specifiedrisk (IRE)*

Trainer: Nicky Henderson

Form: **U1-**

This is a mare that looks to have the ability to go right to the top under rules following her point-to point win. She was sent off the 4/5 favourite on debut but unseated her rider at the second fence. She faced a maximum field of 19 on her second start, in a 5-year-old maiden race for mares, again well fancied and this time justified the market support by scoring in impressive style by 3 ½ lengths. She was subject to huge interest when sent to the sales and Anthony Bromley won that battle on behalf of Robert Waley-Cohen for a staggering £200,000. Theatre Territory should make her presence felt in bumpers and hurdles against her own sex and it is likely that she will make up into a Graded performer in time. If kept to bumpers for the 2015/16 campaign, races such as the Listed bumper at Sandown in March and the Listed Mares bumper at Aintree's Grand National meeting could be on her agenda.

A STEEPLECHASER OF A LIFETIME

Kauto Star - 19.03.2000 – 29.06.2015

Over the close season, National Hunt racing fans mourned the loss of Kauto Star, the greatest steeplechaser of the modern era and described as the best since the mighty Arkle. In a world full of tragedy and disarray, the death of a 15 year old gelding may be insignificant but 'King Kauto' was part of the furniture, a legend that is certain to have left lasting memories for everybody involved.

One feels especially sad for those closest to the horse, the people that will ultimately struggle to come to terms that he is gone. These include owner Clive Smith, former trainer Paul Nicholls and Clifford Baker, the man who looked after him during his racing career and ultimately devoted his working life to this outstanding horse.

Kauto Star was purchased by businessman owner Smith in 2004 for 400,000 Euros in a deal that could be described as 'lucky', with Smith's main target being Garde Champetre until he was outbid by Irish millionaire JP McManus. Maybe it wasn't luck, maybe it was just fate, Kauto was made for Smith and Smith was made for Kauto.

In a career that spanned eight seasons, he made the headlines on numerous occasions with his outstanding performances, capturing an audience that would become his devoted fan base. He was victorious 23 times, amassing over £2m in prize money and proved himself effective over the minimum distance of two miles before progressing into one of the most recognised staying chasers of all time.

Remarkably, his biggest rival Denman lived in the stable next door. Known by many as 'The Tank', Denman's Gold Cup record reads an impressive 1222 and his memorable Cheltenham battles with his old foe Kauto will forever be cherished as a golden era in the staying chase division. Anybody that entered Nicholls' Ditcheat stables while these two warriors were in training must have felt that they were in the presence of greatness.

In years to come, Kauto Star is likely to be remembered as the first horse to regain the Cheltenham Gold Cup (2009) but his record at Kempton was outstanding and it is his record-breaking 5 wins in the King George VI Chase that cements his place in history as a National Hunt great.

A personal highlight was when many felt that he was heading towards retirement before he showed all his old zest to win the Betfair Chase at Haydock for the fourth time in November 2011. That memory will be forever embedded as the moment that my equine hero managed to prove any doubters wrong and establish himself as a steeplechaser of a lifetime.

The last time that I saw Kauto Star in the flesh was at Lambourn during the 2015 open day, where his beautiful white-blazed face was peering out of his box, welcoming all of the visitors to Oliver Sherwood's Rhonehurst stables. Even with the rain beating down and the hundreds of current horses in training to attract people's attention, the onlookers could not help but rush to have their photo taken with the horse that warrants the often over-used term of 'legendary'.

Rest in peace Kauto Star, gone but never forgotten.

BIG RACE ANALYSIS

CHAMPION HURDLE

Last season's Champion Hurdle was all about whether the unbeaten **Faugheen** could make the step up into open company against more experienced rivals. He answered that question to remain unbeaten, capturing the hurdling crown in emphatic style. He rounded his season off at the Punchestown Festival, winning the Grade 1 Punchestown Champion Hurdle, confirming the form with Cheltenham second Arctic Fire and taking his career tally to a perfect ten from ten. The next question is, can Faugheen take on the new challengers and join the greats that have won multiple Champion Hurdles? The answer at this stage is probably yes. At the time of writing the ante-post price of 4/5 reflects that and although he looks like he will be extremely difficult to beat, an ante-post bet at that price is impossible to advise. Faugheen appears to have everything required to become a dual Champion, with his jumping appearing to improve with experience, something that his critics have often questioned. Comparisons with the mighty Istabraq echoed around Prestbury Park following his Champion Hurdle win, a flattering assessment at this early stage but he certainly has what it takes to become a hurdling great and is still the most exciting two mile hurdler in training.

Looking for ante-post value could prove a difficult task in a race where the favourite looks extremely hard to beat. However, the main challenger to Faugheen's crown could be Nicky Henderson's unbeaten juvenile **Peace And Co**, a top prospect for this year's jumps guide and his profile can be read on page 35. The Champion Hurdle is not a great race for 5-year-olds as only one horse aged five has been successful out of the 94 that have tried since 1985. However, Peace And Co looks equipped to cope with the speed challenges of this race and he is expected to make a smooth transition from the juvenile hurdle ranks under the careful tuition of his astute trainer, Henderson. He can be expected to be lightly campaigned during the 2015/16 season and races like the Fighting Fifth at Newcastle, Cheltenham's International Hurdle and

Haydock's Champion Hurdle Trial are highlighted as likely targets. He may face last season's Champion Hurdle fifth **The New One** in any of those encounters, if The New One remain over hurdles in the coming season. That appears unlikely as an imminent switch to fences is expected for that rival following last year's Champion disappointment. It is highly unlikely that we will see Faugheen face Peace And Co in the months leading up to the Champion Hurdle, with Faugheen likely to remain in Ireland and that makes for a mouth-watering race come March.

Supreme Novices' Hurdle winner **Douvan** is fully-expected to take high rank as a novice chaser next season. He was mightily impressive at last season's festival and if he was connected differently we would be wetting our appetite at the potential clash between two hurdling heavy-weights in Faugheen and Douvan. Unfortunately, the racing world is unlikely to ever witness the two face each other. The only way that Douvan would line-up here is in the unfortunate event of anything happening to Faugheen.

Last season's runner-up **Arctic Fire** ran a cracking race in defeat when staying-on best of all to finish 1 ½ lengths behind the winner. His next race came at Aintree in the Grade 1 Aintree Hurdle over 2m4f where he looked the likely winner before taking a heavy fall at the final flight. His final appearance of the season was at the Punchestown Festival, where he was a well-beaten 8 lengths behind easy winner Faugheen. It is likely that his fall at Aintree took its toll and for that reason his effort at Punchestown was understandably below-par. This horse has showed significant improvement throughout the 2014/15 campaign and it will be interesting to see if he can continue on an upward curve next term.

Neptune Novices' Hurdle winner **Windsor Park** would be a worthy contender should he revert back to the minimum distance next season. The roll of honour for Neptune winners who have followed up in the Champion Hurdle include Hardy Eustace, multiple-champion Istabraq and most recently Faugheen. With two obvious festival targets looking likely at this stage (Champion or World Hurdle), it is difficult to advise Dermot Weld's gelding as a real Champion Hurdle contender. However, as the Neptune Novices' Hurdle is often a good pointer to the following season's Champion, this horse cannot be ruled out at this early stage.

Jezki and **My Tent Or Yours** were first and second in the 2014 renewal. Jezki is likely to remain over three miles following his victory at Punchestown and My Tent Or Yours has been off the track with a minor tendon injury which is hardly ideal preparation. However, he would deserve the ultimate respect if he is back to the form of his good second to Jezki and the current price of 33/1 is a tempting each-way bet.

Another Nicky Henderson inmate that looks over-priced at this stage is **Top Notch**, currently trading at 40/1. He ran an excellent race to finish second behind the selection Peace And Co in the Triumph Hurdle and although he looks destined to make up into a chaser in time, given the opportunity, he could prove to be a lively outsider.

Shaneshill was a runner-up behind Douvan in the Supreme Novices' Hurdle in 2015 and although he looks to have a bit to find on ratings, he still rates as a promising young hurdler.

His stablemate, **Nicholls Canyon**, a four-time Grade 1 winning novice hurdler during the 2014/15 campaign, would not look out of place in a Champion Hurdle as he possesses the speed and attitude that is required. However, he looks best suited to more of a stamina test and the World Hurdle looks his number one aim at next season's festival.

SELECTION: Peace And Co   **DANGER:** Faugheen

CHAMPION CHASE

The championship race for two-mile chasers has a stellar list of former National Hunt greats including Moscow Flyer, Master Minded, Sizing Europe and most recently Sprinter Sacre.

Last season's race ended in heartbreak for National Hunt fans as former champion Sprinter Sacre was pulled-up when out of contention turning into the straight.

However, that does not decry the excellent performance of **Dodging Bullets**, who was winning his third Grade 1 prize of the season for champion trainer Paul Nicholls. Over the course of the 2014/15 season, Dodging Bullets finally displayed the natural ability that he possesses. He reappeared in a Listed chase at Cheltenham, where he finished a 2 length third behind subsequent Ryanair Chase winner Uxizandre. He appeared to benefit from his seasonal reappearance and ran out an impressive winner of the Grade 1 Tingle Creek Chase at Sandown on his next start, beating the ultra-consistent Somersby by 2 ½ lengths. All eyes were on Sprinter Sacre in the Grade 1 Clarence House Chase at Ascot as he made his comeback after being found with an irregular heartbeat back in 2013 but it was Dodging Bullets who stole the headlines, with an easy 3 length victory. Given his excellent Grade 1 form, it was remarkable that he was sent off the 9/2 third favourite in the Champion Chase, where he again repelled the late challenge of Somersby to win by 1 ¼ lengths. Although he is sure to compete in the Grade 1 two-mile chases during the 2015/16 campaign, it remains to be seen whether he will be good enough to retain his crown at the 2016 festival, especially with an outstanding novice chaser from last season likely to prove very hard to beat.

That outstanding novice is the Willie Mullins-trained **Un De Sceaux** who looks to be a two-mile chaser with the world at his feet and is the one that they all have to beat at this early stage. He is a best priced 6/4 favourite at the time of writing and although an ante-post wager is not advised, he is certain to be shorter come March if his second season over fences goes as expected. He has raced five times over fences, winning four and falling once when miles clear at Thurles on his chase debut. He destroyed subsequent Grade 1 winner Clarcam by 15 lengths at Leopardstown in January, before he announced himself as the best two-mile novice chaser in training at the Cheltenham Festival. He was an impressive 6 length winner at the festival, beating Grade 1 winning chaser God's Own in the Grade 1 Arkle Challenge Trophy. Arkle winners have an excellent record when attempting to win the Champion Chase in the following season with Moscow Flyer (2003), Voy Por Ustedes (2007), Sizing Europe (2011) and Sprinter Sacre (2013) all successfully completing the double in recent years. The sky really is the limit for this 7-year-old and he ranks as one of the most exciting horses in training.

Previous Champion Chase hero **Sprinter Sacre** looks a shadow of his former self and it is impossible to advise him as potential winner of this race at this stage. Every National Hunt racing fan cherishes the performances that Nicky Henderson's gelding blessed us with between 2011 and 2013 and if he was able to return to his awesome best, he would be a sure fire winner of Grade 1 chases over two-miles in 2015/16 season.

Un De Sceaux's stablemate **Vautour** was a simply breathtaking winner of the JLT Novices' Chase at the 2015 Cheltenham Festival, where he beat Apache Stronghold and subsequent Grade 1 winner Valseur Lido by 15 lengths. Given the opportunity, he has the speed and class to challenge his awesome stablemate but it remains unlikely that we will see the two face each other over fences. Connections appear most likely to gear Vautour's campaign around either the Ryanair Chase or the Cheltenham Gold Cup at the 2016 festival, with a drop back to the minimum trip for the Champion Chase seeming unlikely at this stage.

Sire De Grugy deserves a mention with his greatest success to date coming in this race in 2014. Being a 9-year-old it seems doubtful that he will be able to re-capture his very best form, the form that is required for him to compete with the likes of Un De Sceaux. However, he should continue to prove himself capable of competing at Grade 1 level in Britain, where the two-mile chase division appears to be lacking a real superstar.

Two-time Cheltenham Festival winner **Champagne Fever** has an excellent record around Prestbury Park with his form figures reading 112 and he rates as a lively outsider at this stage. He was pulled out on the day of last season's Champion Chase, after failing to recover from a minor injury. If you can forgive him a dismal effort at Punchestown when he was beaten 30 lengths, his record over two miles in bumpers, over hurdles and over fences is first-class. He all but won the Grade 1 Arkle Challenge Trophy at the Cheltenham Festival in 2014 and if he can produce his best form next March, the 25/1 that is currently available would be an excellent each-way bet.

Of the remainder **God's Own** and **Special Tiara** would be two to consider as horses with each-way possibilities. God's Own was second to Un De Sceaux in the Grade 1 Arkle Challenge Trophy and showed an excellent attitude on the run-in to be beaten 6 lengths in the end. He will need to improve his jumping as this has let him down on numerous occasions but he has scope for further improvement as a chaser. Special Tiara was an impressive winner on his latest start at Sandown, beating Sprinter Sacre by 6 lengths in the Grade 1 Celebration Chase. He has a solid enough looking profile with a third in last season's Champion Chase and given a soft lead he often proves very hard to pass.

SELECTION: Un De Sceaux   **DANGER:** Dodging Bullets

WORLD HURDLE

The World Hurdle has been dominated in recent years by Big Buck's, an outstanding staying hurdler and one whose record of four wins in the race is unlikely to be surpassed. Baracouda was successful in the 2002 and 2003 renewals before finishing runner-up in 2004 and 2005 and Inglis Drever dominated this division with three wins between 2005 and 2008, confirming that this is a race where former winners have an excellent record.

With the above considered, there is no better starting place than last season's champion, **Cole Harden**. Warren Greatrex's stable star proved himself as a useful novice hurdler during the 2013/14 campaign, most notably when an excellent second to Beat That in the Grade 1 Sefton Novices' Hurdle at Aintree. He confirmed his early promise when winning on his seasonal reappearance last season in Wetherby's Grade 2 Bet365 Hurdle (registered as the West Yorkshire Hurdle), beating Medinas by a comfortable 8 lengths. That rival reversed the form at Newbury in the Grade 2 Long Distance Hurdle, this time in receipt of 8lbs, in a race where the ground conditions were very different to Wetherby. Cole Harden then put up two decent efforts at Cheltenham where he was third behind Rock On Ruby before finishing a 16 length fourth behind Saphir Du Rheu in the Grade 2 Cleeve Hurdle. He returned to Prestbury Park for the Grade 1 World Hurdle and was sent off at 14/1 to be crowned the champion staying hurdler. It was reported pre-race that the horse had undergone a wind operation and it appeared to make all the difference as he exceeded his previous efforts with a brilliant display of front-running. He showed an excellent attitude that day, bounding clear up the hill to win by 3 ¼ lengths, reversing the form with his Cleeve Hurdle conqueror, Saphir Du Rheu. He closed the season with another good performance, this time finishing 3 ½ lengths behind Whisper in the Grade 1 Stayers' Hurdle at Aintree. After a long season it is possible that he was below his best at Aintree. Having said that, the winner appeared to improve for the run at Cheltenham and Cole Harden remains a very exciting staying hurdle prospect for the 2015/16 campaign.

Former Champion Hurdle winner **Jezki** announced himself as a potential superstar in the staying hurdle division at the end of last season. This 7-year-old was previously one of the leading two-milers in training but following an 8 ¼ length defeat in last season's Champion Hurdle, connections opted to step him up in trip for the Grade 1 Aintree Hurdle. He was perhaps a fortunate winner with Arctic Fire travelling powerfully before taking a heavy fall at the final flight. His 13 length success that day made him two from two over the 2m4f trip, justifying why connections are excited about the prospects of him establishing himself as a top-class staying hurdler. Jezki tackled three miles for the first time at Punchestown and made no mistake in defeating his old foe and two-time Champion Hurdle winner Hurricane Fly by 1 ¾ lengths. This was a monumental race between two outstanding hurdlers, neither of which were easy to settle in the early stages and the winners stamina was what counted in the final couple of furlongs. Now he has proved that he stays the three mile trip, he is sure to continue his career in excess of two miles and looks a lively candidate for the World Hurdle in 2016. If he is able to settle better in his races, he could be an exceptional staying hurdler and it is likely that connections will opt for the hood, an aid that was used for the first time when triumphant in the 2014 Champion Hurdle. His Cheltenham record over hurdles reads 314, all in Grade 1 races and he has the pedigree to make his presence felt in the most prestigious race for staying hurdlers.

More Of That was an impressive winner of the 2014 renewal of the World Hurdle and assuming that he returns in the same form after a frustrating 2014/15 season, JP McManus' new stable jockey Barry Geraghty will have a difficult decision to choose between Jezki and More Of That in early March. Unbeaten in five career starts, he made his seasonal reappearance in the Grade 2 Long Distance Hurdle at Newbury where he was sent off the 4/7 favourite and eventually finished a disappointing 25 length third. It was far from ideal that he had to chase the race-fit Cole Harden, who set a good gallop in testing ground and therefore it was understandable that he appeared to get tired in the closing stages of the race. His World Hurdle win came on good ground and after his Newbury defeat, it is concluded that he is best suited to faster ground conditions when tackling three miles. He was not seen again after Newbury and the fact that he wore a tongue tie for the first time that day may hint that he has a minor breathing issue. It is hoped that Jonjo O'Neill will have resolved any issues over the summer and given that he has already shown that he is a top-class staying hurdler when the conditions are in his favour, he should take the beating in a good ground renewal. The 12/1 that is on offer at this early stage looks decent value as he could be considerably shorter once he confirms his well-being.

Of the remainder, Neptune Novices' Hurdle winner **Windsor Park** makes most appeal with a step up to three miles being considered for this Dermot Weld-trained gelding. He is yet to race beyond the 2m5f that he encountered in the Neptune at the Cheltenham Festival but he wasn't stopping at the line and he will warrant the ultimate respect if his connections opt to go down the staying hurdling route. He is lightly raced over hurdles, operating at a 50% strike rate (two wins from four) so further improvement is expected from this 6-year-old son of Galileo.

Multiple Grade 1-winning novice hurdler **Nichols Canyon** warrants a mention after an excellent first season over hurdles. His owner has been successful three times in this race with Inglis Drever and given the opportunity, this Willie Mullins-trained gelding could take some stopping if he can prove he stays the three mile trip. However, he looks a 2m4f specialist and it is likely that his main spring target will be the Aintree Hurdle at the Grand National meeting.

The other horses at the head of the betting look certain to take up different engagements at the 2016 festival including **Annie Power**. She was an excellent second in the 2014 renewal behind the selection More Of That, proving that she stays the three mile trip and she would be well-fancied to go one better given the chance. However, the Grade 1 Mares Hurdle looks likely to be her festival target again this time around where she will take all the beating on official ratings. A number of other horses that could easily be considered for the World Hurdle in 2016 look certain to continue their careers over the larger obstacles as novice chasers. These include top prospects, **Whisper**, **Saphir Du Rheu** and **Thistlecrack** as well as the 2015 Albert Bartlett winner **Martello Tower**. In a race that may lack strength in depth come March, any of the aforementioned horses would warrant consideration but their participation appears unlikely.

SELECTION: More Of That   **DANGER:** Jezki

THE CHELTENHAM GOLD CUP

The Cheltenham Gold Cup, the most prestigious prize in National Hunt racing and one which many owners and trainers dream of winning, with very few successfully achieving the great feat.

Last year's renewal promised to be an excellent encounter, billed as the old versus the new, with a number of smart second season chasers attempting to take on seasoned campaigners including 2014 hero Lord Windermere and 2013 champion and multiple festival winner Bob's Worth. However, the most remarkable story of the entire race was the prospect of a novice chaser, who had only raced three times over fences, attempting to win steeplechasing's blue-ribbon event. That horse was the Mark Bradstock-trained 8-year-old Coneygree and he managed to capture the hearts of the entire National Hunt family by defying the odds to become the first horse since Irish champion Captain Christy triumphed in 1974 to win the Cheltenham Gold Cup as a novice.

The reigning champion **Coneygree** has to be the first horse to be mentioned in the preview of the 2016 renewal after making history in last season's race and looking like a superstar of the staying ranks. He remarkably only made his debut over fences in November 2014 at Newbury, less than four months before his Gold Cup assignment. He was upped in class on his second start for the Grade 1 Kauto Star Novices' Chase (formerly known as the Feltham Novices' Chase) where he was extremely impressive, winning by 40 lengths, even if the race did fall apart with Saphir Du Rheu, Sausalito Sunrise and Carraig Mor all coming to grief. He faced seasoned chasers on his third start at Newbury in the Grade 2 Denman Chase where he retained his unbeaten record over the larger obstacles, beating ultra-consistent Houblon Des Obeaux by 7 lengths. It was that performance that had connections dreaming of Gold Cup glory, with the RSA chase previously considered as the end of season target. As Cheltenham week arrived, connections made the decision to let their evidently smart novice chaser take on the very best steeplechasers in training in the Cheltenham Gold Cup. A brilliant front-running display, jumping tremendously throughout and showed a willing attitude after the last to get the better of Djakadam by 1 ½ lengths. His win in the Denman Chase merited his participation in this race and although the rain came at the perfect time for Coneygree, he remains one of the brightest stars in the staying division. He is sure to be a contender in 2016, with the experience to call upon now, although it appears that there a number of formidable opponents to challenge him once more.

Gold Cup runner-up **Djakadam** is a worthy contender for the 2016 renewal after his fantastic second, a fine-effort for another lightly-raced chaser. Previously unbeaten in two novice chases, he was travelling well in the 2014 JLT Novices' Chase at the festival before crashing out with four left to jump, leaving the impression that he was a promising sort for the future. He was the well-backed favourite for the Hennessey on his seasonal reappearance where he caught the eye for a long way before getting tired in the closing stages. His stamina was reportedly questioned post-race but he confirmed his promise as a staying chaser when running out an impressive 8 length winner of the Thyestes Handicap Chase at Gowran Park in January. He was sent of a fancied 10/1 for the Gold Cup in March following his Gowran success and ran a gallant race to finish a close second to Coneygree. He bumped into another smart-chaser at Punchestown where he finished 7 lengths behind Don Cossack, confirming the Gold Cup form with Road To Riches 6 ½ lengths back in third. This 6-year-old has time on his side and further improvement is expected from this Willie Mullins-trained gelding. The Gold Cup is a tough test, so it is a concern that Djakadam has encountered the race so early on in his career. However, at this early stage, it seems likely that he will be able to turn the form with his Gold Cup conqueror after an excellent second season as a chaser and he remains a very bright prospect in the staying chase division.

Paul Nicholls' **Saphir Du Rheu** started last season as one of the most promising novice chasers in training. He fell on his chase debut at Exeter before following up at the same venue, beating Horizontal Speed by 11 lengths. He again fell on his third start, this time in the Grade 1 Kauto Star

Novices' Chase (formerly known as the Feltham Novices' Chase). He was reverted back to hurdles at an attempt to boost his confidence and won the Cleeve Hurdle at Cheltenham at the first time of asking. He took his chance in the World Hurdle on his second hurdle start of the season and ran an encouraging race to finish second behind the excellent Cole Harden. Nicholls has always held this horse in extremely high-regard, highlighting him a potential superstar over fences so it was no surprise to see Saphir Du Rheu switched back to the larger obstacles for the Grade 1 Mildmay Novices' Chase. He travelled well throughout, jumping with plenty of fluency and was a run-away winner in the end, beating Carraig Mor by an easy 15 lengths. This 6-year-old looks a stayer with a big future over fences and the 20-1 that is currently available is good value at this early stage.

RSA Chase winner **Don Poli** rates an exciting prospect for this season after he put up an excellent display at last season's festival scoring in the manner of a real stayer. His win at Cheltenham was following two successes across the Irish Sea, first at Gowran on his debut where he was a comfortable winner before landing the Grade 1 Topaz Novices' Chase at Leopardstown. His latest run at the Punchestown Festival was a real disappointing effort but after a hard race in the RSA, this can be forgiven. This horse appears to have stamina to burn and that is a trait that is required to be considered a genuine Gold Cup contender. Although he is not advised as the winner at this stage, he is sure to be involved next March.

Current ante-post favourite **Vautour** is a really exciting second season chaser after winning the JLT in stunning fashion last term. If he is stepped up in trip by Willie Mullins then he is certain to be feared by all. He has a high cruising speed and an economical jumping technique that will stand him in good stead if connections opt to go down the staying chase route. It is likely that his stamina will be tested in the King George VI Chase at Kempton and the result of that race will form his spring targets. At this stage, with connections strong hand in this race, the Ryanair looks the most likely spring target for Vautour but it would be no surprise if he did show up in the Gold Cup and given the opportunity, he would take a lot of beating.

Don Cossack had an excellent 2014/15 season with six wins from seven chase starts, his only defeat coming in the 2015 Ryanair Chase at the festival. Although he was an impressive winner on his latest start at the Punchestown Festival over 3m1f, the stamina sapping 3m2f at Cheltenham is unlikely to prove ideal for Gordon Elliott's gelding. He appears to be best suited by races over 2m4f and 2m5f and for that reason, he looks likely to try and make amends for his defeat in last season's Ryanair Chase.

Of the remainder, last season's third-placed **Road To Riches** makes little appeal as he looks firmly held by Coneygree and Djakadam on last season's run. Grand National winner **Many Clouds** would have an each-way chance after proving himself an excellent staying chaser last term which also included wins in the Hennessey at Newbury and in a Grade 2 at Cheltenham in January. **Holywell's** chances appear to hinge on the ground conditions as he has proved himself a much better performer when tackling good ground and he could be a forgotten horse come March if conditions were in his favour.

SELECTION: Saphir Du Rheu   **DANGER:** Djakadam

INDEX OF HORSES

VERY WOOD, 20, 58, 66
VICTOR HEWGO, 65
VOLNAY DE THAIX, 46

WELSH SHADOW, 47
WEST WIZARD, 67
WHISPER, 45, 48-49
WILLIAM HENRY, 50

YANWORTH, 41, 51
YORKHILL, 33, 52-53, 71

ZUBAYR, 54

Printed in Great Britain
by Amazon.co.uk, Ltd.,
Marston Gate.